Advance Praise for Amy James's Knowledge Esse

"Knowledge Essentials is a remarkable series that will benefit children of all abilities and learning styles. Amy James has taken a close look at curriculum standards and testing around the country and developed simple and creative activities that support what's being taught at each grade level, while remaining sensitive to the fact that children learn at different rates and in different ways. I highly recommend it for all parents who want to make a difference in their children's education."

—Michael Gurian, author of *Boys and Girls Learn Differently* and *The Wonder of Boys*

"Finally, a book about teaching young children by somebody who knows her stuff! I can (and will) wholeheartedly recommend this series to the ever-growing number of parents who ask me for advice about how they can help their children succeed in elementary school."

—LouAnne Johnson, author of *Dangerous Minds* and *The Queen of Education*

"Having examined state standards nationwide, Amy James has created innovative and unique games and exercises to help children absorb what they *have* to learn, in ways that will help them *want* to learn. Individualized to the child's own learning style, this is a must-have series for parents who want to maximize their child's ability to succeed in and out of the class-room."

—Myrna B. Shure, Ph.D., author of *Thinking Parents, Thinking Child*

"The books in Amy James's timely and unique Knowledge Essentials series give parents a clear idea of what their children are learning and provide the tools they need to help their children live up to their full academic potential. This is must reading for any parent with a school-age child."

—Michele Borba, Ed.D., author of *Nobody Likes Me, Everybody Hates Me* and *No More Misbehavin'*

KE™ KNOWLEDGE ESSENTIALS™

PRESCHOOL SUCCESS

Everything You Need to Know to Help Your Child Learn

AMY JAMES

JOSSEY-BASS
A Wiley Imprint
www.josseybass.com

Published by Jossey-Bass
A Wiley Imprint
989 Market Street, San Francisco, CA 94103-1741
www.josseybass.com

Excerpt in Chapter Twelve is from Irene Daria, "Help Your Preschooler Handle Frustration," Copyright © 2004. Reprinted with permission from the November 2000 issue of *Parents* magazine.

Limit of Liability/Disclaimer of Warranty: While the publisher and author have used their best efforts in preparing this book, they make no representations or warranties with respect to the accuracy or completeness of the contents of this book and specifically disclaim any implied warranties of merchantability or fitness for a particular purpose. No warranty may be created or extended by sales representatives or written sales materials. The advice and strategies contained herein may not be suitable for your situation. You should consult with a professional where appropriate. Neither the publisher nor author shall be liable for any loss of profit or any other commercial damages, including but not limited to special, incidental, consequential, or other damages.

Readers should be aware that Internet Web sites offered as citations and/or sources for further information may have changed or disappeared between the time this was written and when it is read.

Permission is given for individual classroom teachers to reproduce the pages and illustrations for classroom use. Reproduction of these materials for an entire school system is strictly forbidden.

Jossey-Bass books and products are available through most bookstores. To contact Jossey-Bass directly call our Customer Care Department within the U.S. at 800-956-7739, outside the U.S. at 317-572-3986, or fax 317-572-4002.

Jossey-Bass also publishes its books in a variety of electronic formats. Some content that appears in print may not be available in electronic books.

Library of Congress Cataloging-in-Publication Data

James, Amy, date.
  Preschool success: everything you need to know to help your child learn / Amy James.
      p. cm.—(Knowledge essentials)
  Includes bibliographical references and index.
  ISBN-13: 978-0-471-74814-4 (pbk.)
  ISBN-10: 0-471-74814-5 (pbk.)
  1. Education, Preschool—Curricula—United States. 2. Education, Preschool—Parent participation. I. Title. II. Series. III. Series: James, Amy, 1967– Knowledge essentials
  LB1140.4.J36 2006
  372.21—dc22
                                                                                      2006010539

Printed in the United States of America
FIRST EDITION
PB Printing 10 9 8 7 6 5 4 3 2 1

To Richard Harroch, a great boss, fabulous mentor, and good friend.
Thanks for submitting my book proposal!

CONTENTS

ACKNOWLEDGMENTS

I would like to thank the following people for advising me on this book:

Cindy King is a retired early childhood and reading specialist who taught kindergarten and first grade for thirty years. She assisted in establishing the transition program at her school district, a program for children who are developmentally young.

E. W. James was an elementary school principal and elementary school teacher for fifteen years. He led the school district's efforts to serve children with special needs.

Elizabeth Hecox is in her sixteenth year of teaching at Kennedy Elementary School in Norman, Oklahoma. She is an incredible classroom teacher, and the book is better because of her work with me on it.

Kim Lindsay is in her twelfth year of teaching elementary school in Dallas Public Schools and in Norman Public Schools. She was elected Teacher of the Year at Kennedy Elementary School in the 2001–2002 school year.

Pam Davidson retired from Norman Public Schools after spending 15 years in the classroom and 10 years as an elementary school principal. Pam has been a valued family friend for over 30 years and I am grateful that she is here to help me with this book series.

The employees at Six Things, Inc., are a group of thirty current and former teachers who provide invaluable assistance on a daily basis. Anytime I needed help in any subject area, for any grade, their enormously good brains were at my disposal. This book series would not be possible without their assistance, and I am eternally grateful to them for their help.

Introduction

Welcome to the first step toward your child's higher education: preschool. Do you live in a community with competitive preschool admissions? Is your preschool application more detailed than a law school application? When did early childhood become about developmental indicators, benchmark tests, and cognitive learning? Is a teaching certificate a prerequisite for helping your child learn? When did preschool become so complicated?

Parents want what's best for their child, so it's easy to get wrapped up with competition, peer pressure, and performance standards. Relax, calm down, and stay in control. Home is the single most important learning environment your child will have, and parents are the single most important teachers. You and the learning environment you create in your home need to accommodate your child's growth and increasing skill levels.

As a parent, you are a primary caregiver, role model, and provider. Your preschooler looks to you as the final authority; the last word; the smartest, strongest, prettiest, or most handsome person he or she knows. Learning environments are important. Whether your child is at school, at home, or in the car, the way you interact with your little learner will influence his or her abilities for a lifetime.

To effectively enhance your child's learning, you need to be constantly and consistently aware of your child's development over the years so that you can come to know his or her particular strengths, shortcomings, and areas of talent and natural inclination. And just because you know one of your children does not mean you know them all. Children's minds differ substantially from their siblings'. Each child is his or her own person with a unique set of abilities. As you gain insights into your children's development, you can easily help each child strengthen abilities while closing any important gaps or concentrating on areas of difficulty.

An academically progressive home life is the key to effectively tracking your child's development as well as providing opportunities to successfully apply knowledge. Creating the environment is not about tutoring but about creating opportunities to learn and apply learning. The point is to bring the level of content and conversation in your daily life to the level that is in your child's school life. Home, your child's first learning environment, is the primary testing ground for new knowledge and skill sets.

Getting the Most from This Book

This book is a guide to creating an exceptional learning environment in your home. It contains curricula and skills unique to preschool presented in a way that makes it easy to put what you learn into practice. This book serves as a tool to help solve the mystery behind creating a supportive, learning-rich environment in your home that fosters a thinking child's development while enriching his or her curricula. It contains dozens of mini–lesson plans that include easy-to-use activities designed to help your child meet your state's learning requirements. An environmental learning section in each chapter tells you how to identify learning opportunities in the everyday world.

Chapters 2 through 4 give you some child development information to get you started. Teaching is about knowing the subject area you teach, but moreover it is about knowing the abilities of the students you teach. As a parent you can easily see the milestones your child reaches at an early age (crawling, walking, talking, and so on), but milestones are not always apparent in your four- to five-year-old. These chapters explain the child development processes that take place during preschool, including what thinking milestones your child's brain is capable of and will reach in normal development during this time. In order for you to teach effectively, you will need to account for these developmental milestones in all topics and skills that you introduce.

Teaching is also about recognizing how different people learn and tailoring the way you teach to suit them. You will find out how to recognize different learning styles in chapter 3, which will help you implement the learning activities in the rest of the book.

Chapters 5 through 10 provide general subject area information for preschool curricula. The curricula discussed in this book were chosen by reviewing all fifty of the state learning standards, the National Subject Area Association learning standards, the core curriculum materials that many school districts use, and supplemental education products. Although there are some discrepancies in curricula from region to region, they are few and far between. Chances are that even if you aren't able to use all of the topical subject area units (such as social studies and science), you will be able to use most of them. Reading, writing, and math are skill-based subjects that are chosen according to specific child development indicators, particularly in preschool. It is likely that you will be able to use all the information in those chapters. Each chapter provides learning activities that you can do at home with your child.

Chapter 11 discusses assessment: How do teachers tell if your child is learning? What are the different ways to tell if your child is learning? Chapter 11 answers those questions and those you may have about assessment. The focus of chapter 12 is understanding how your child is developing from a social perspective. Chapter 13 discusses how your child will demonstrate that he or she is prepared for kindergarten. The appendixes provide information on products that meet certain preschool learning needs.

You won't read this book from cover to cover while lounging on the beach. I hope it will be a raggedy, dog-eared, marked-up book that has been thumbed through, spilled on, and referred to throughout the school year. Here are some tips on using this book:

Do

- Use this book as a reference guide throughout your child's preschool year.
- Model activities and approaches after the information you find in this book when creating your own supplemental learning activities.
- Modify the information to meet your needs and your child's needs.

Don't

- Complete the activities in this book from beginning to end. Instead, mix and match them appropriately to the curriculum and/or skills your child is learning in school.
- Use this book as a homeschool curriculum. It will help with your homeschooling in the same way it helps parents who don't homeschool—it supplements the preschool core curriculum.
- Challenge your child's teacher on the basis of information you find here. ("Why isn't my child writing the first letter of her name, as it said she should in *Preschool Success?*") Instead, look for the synergy in the information from both sources.

Use this book and its resources as supplemental information to enhance your child's preschool curriculum—and let's make it a good year for everyone!

Getting the Most for Your Preschooler

1

No parent says, "Oh, mediocre is okay for my child. Please do things halfway; it doesn't matter." Parents want the best for their children. This is not a matter of spending the most money on education or buying the latest great educational toy. It is a matter of spending time with your child and expending effort to maximize what he or she is being provided by the school, by the community, and at home.

Getting the Most from Your Preschool

You wouldn't think twice about getting the most bang for your buck from a hotel, your gym, or a restaurant, and you shouldn't think twice about getting the most from your child's preschool.

Public Preschools

"What?" you say? Public preschools? Yes, it's a new day, and there are public preschools and established preschool learning goals for sixteen states and counting. If your state has public preschools, then you are in luck—financially and educationally. In these states, preschools fall under the leadership of your State Department of Education. (You can find a complete list of states with public preschools at www. knowledgeessentials.com.) This means they are subject to the same regulations and standards that your public schools are and that your area's preschools are poised to prepare your child for kindergarten.

To further your child's educational experience, you will have the opportunity to meet and work with:

- School personnel: your child's teacher, teacher's aides, specialists, the school counselor, the administrator or principal, and others
- Parents of children from your child's class, school volunteers, and parent–teacher organizations

Your participation in your child's education is paramount to his or her success. Active participation doesn't mean that you have to spend hours at the school as a volunteer, but it does include reading all the communications your school sends either to you directly or home with your child. Also, read the school handbook and drop by your child's school on a regular basis if possible. If you can't stop by, check out the school or class Web site to see what units are being covered, any upcoming events, and so on. Participation means attending school events when you can, going to class parties when possible, and going to parent–teacher conferences. If they are scheduled at a time when you are not available, request a different time. The school administrator or principal usually requires that teachers try to accommodate your schedule.

The single most important thing you can do to get the most out of your local school system is to talk to your child's teacher. Find out what curricula your child will be covering and how you can help facilitate learning. Does the teacher see specific strengths and weaknesses that you can help enhance or bring up to speed? The teacher can help you identify your child's learning style, social skills, problem-solving abilities, and coping mechanisms.

Teachers play a role that extends outside the classroom. Your child's teacher is the perfect person to recommend systemwide and community resources. Teachers know how to find local playgroups, good summer programs, and community resources. You've heard of Spanish immersion classes for preschoolers but don't know where to find them? Ask your child's preschool teacher. Art classes for the very young? Same thing. Teachers are truly partners in your child's upbringing.

No matter what, active participation and communication with your child's school is essential. It empowers you to:

- Accurately monitor your child's progress

- Determine which optional activities would enrich your child's learning experience

- Prepare your child for upcoming events, curricula, and skill introduction

- Participate in and add to the school learning environment

- Create a complementary learning environment in your home

- Spend time with your child

And just a word about the school secretary: this person knows more about what is going on in that building than anyone else. When I was a teacher, the school secretary always added to my success and that of my students. The secretary is a taskmaster, nurse, mom or dad, and generally just a comforting figure in what can sometimes be a really big building. The school secretary always knows what forms to fill out, which teacher is where, what students are absent and why, when the next school event is, and how much candy money you owe for the latest fund-raiser. He or she is a source of lunch money, milk money, extra pencils, and access to the copy machine. Get to know and love your school secretary.

Private Preschools

The first thing you need to do is be a smart consumer: choose your child's preschool with the same care you would use in making any major purchase. Here are some tips:

- Start early! It may take longer than you think. You wouldn't want to end up putting your child in a preschool that is just okay, or with plans to move your child to another facility when you "find a better one." Your child will make friends, bond with the teacher, and generally settle into his new routine. Don't diminish his progress by moving him from preschool to preschool.

- Research! Start finding out as much as you can about the preschools in your area as soon as possible.

- Talk to other parents to see what preschool their children attend and if they are happy with the service and education their children receive.

- Visit a handful of preschools on your short list and compare their environments.

What to Look For in a Preschool

One of the best things you can do when choosing a preschool is to make on-site visits. You can observe firsthand how the children interact with their teachers and classmates while seeing what the setup is inside the classroom. Ask questions and find out all the information you can about the preschool. Even if it seems like the perfect school, you may discover something that could change your mind. For example, maybe there are too many children in each classroom, or maybe your preschooler has to be 100 percent potty trained. Also keep in mind that preschool tuition can vary drastically. This information could quickly change your options. The best thing to do is to make an initial visit to the school without your child and have a list of questions you plan to ask. If you like the preschool and believe it will meet your family's needs, take your child for a visit. Make sure to watch your child and note her reaction to the school. Her reaction may be just as big of a deciding factor as class size or tuition. Before you come to a final decision, make sure you have spoken with both the teachers and the director of the school and that all your questions have been adequately answered.

Here is a list of questions you may want to ask:

What is the tuition?

What about the curriculum? How is it taught? Is the school accredited? Is there a religious affiliation?

How long have the teachers taught at the school? What is their education level? What is the turnover rate? (You don't want your child to have three different preschool teachers in one year.)

Does the building have security? How old is the building, and what kind of shape is it in?

Is there a playground outside? Is there a play area inside?

Will your child only have one teacher? Will he be in one classroom for the entire school day, or is there more than one class?

What is the student–teacher ratio?

How many children will be in one class?

Does each teacher have a teacher's aide?

Is there a school policy manual you can view?

What is the "sick child" policy?

What does the school do about discipline?

Is the program a half day or full day?

Are you responsible for providing your child's lunch and snacks?

What are the toilet training policies?

Are the classrooms child-friendly and well kept?

Are there toys and books for the children?

Will there be any music or art programs?

Will there be any field trips, and if so, what safety policies are in place?

What is the age range of the children in the school? Will your child ever be around older children?

This is just a sampling of the questions you may have about preschools. Remember, not all preschools will be accredited, and not all will have teachers who have a formal education. The importance of these issues is something you will need to decide for yourself and your child. Sometimes a school's reputation may outweigh its credentials, or vice versa. Just because a school has been highly recommended to you or is where your child's friends are going does not mean that the school is right for your child. Because this is your child's first experience with school, it is important that you feel comfortable with your choice and know that your child will be well cared for. You should never choose a preschool based on someone else's opinion—always check it out for yourself!

On a micro level, participating in your child's education if he attends a private school isn't much different from participating if he attends a public school. Private schools have access to the same community resources. If you have a child with special needs, the private school should work with the local education agencies to see that your child gets the appropriate services.

Through active communication and participation, you will derive the same benefits as parents whose children attend public school.

On a macro level, private schools are different from public schools. Private schools are governed not by a school board but by an internal system. This can be both easier and harder to navigate. Dealing with private schools is easier because the schools realize that you are paying tuition every month, and they want to please their customers. Dealing with private schools is harder because they aren't accountable to the community for their actions, nor are they governed by the same due processes as the public school system. Check out the school's administration hierarchy to see how decisions are made and what roles have been created for parent governance. Also, get to know the school's secretary.

For you to really be on top of things, it's a good idea to print a copy of your state's learning standards (see chapter 4) and familiarize yourself with the topics and skills that your state thinks preschoolers should learn. You can find a copy at www.knowledgeessentials.com. Compare the standards to those of your private school's preschool curriculum. If the curriculum is drastically different from the required state learning standards, your child will have difficulty passing the required state assessments. If your child's curriculum meets and exceeds the standards, your child will be well served by that school.

Private schools have the flexibility to incorporate religious elements or varied teaching philosophies that public schools can't provide. They are not subject to requirements regarding the separation of church and state. Private schools operate without depending on community support (such as bond proposals); so as long as their tuition-paying constituency approves of their methods and the students who graduate from the programs demonstrate success, private schools can implement teaching methods at will that fall out of the mainstream.

Getting the Most from Your Homeschool Curriculum

You are homeschooling your child because you want more control over what and how your child learns and the environment in which she learns it. That is admirable, but don't be fooled. To a large extent, your child's natural ability to learn certain things at certain times will dictate the way you should approach any homeschool curriculum (chapters 2 and 3 explain this more fully). The best thing you can do when starting to homeschool your child is to look at books on child development. Start with these:

- *Children's Strategies: Contemporary Views of Cognitive Development,* edited by David F. Bjorklund. Mahwah, N.J.: Erlbaum Associates, 1990.

- *Piaget's Theory: Prospects and Possibilities,* edited by Harry Beilin. Mahwah, N.J.: Erlbaum Associates, 1992.

- *Instructional Theories in Action: Lessons Illustrating Selected Theories and Models,* edited by Charles M. Reigeluth. Mahwah, N.J.: Erlbaum Associates, 1987.

- *All Our Children Learning,* Benjamin S. Bloom. New York: McGraw-Hill, 1981.

You don't have to homeschool your child all by yourself or by limiting yourself to the materials of a particular homeschool organization. Each state has some form of regional education system with centers open to the public. At your public school system's curriculum resource center, you can check out curriculum materials and supplemental materials. Most of these centers have a workroom with things like a die press that cuts out letters and various shapes, from squares to animals to holiday items. Regional education centers often provide continuing education for teachers, so they usually have some training materials on hand. Look for information about your regional center on the Web site of your State Department of Education. You can find a link to your State Department of Education at www.knowledgeessentials.com.

You can purchase homeschool curriculum kits designed to provide your child with a lion's share of the materials needed to complete a grade level—even for preschool. You can also buy curricula that are subject area specific. It is important to ask the company that sells the curricula to correlate the materials with your state's learning standards so that you can see which standards you need to reinforce with additional activities. You can find the companies that sell these kits at www.knowledgeessentials.com.

Using Supplemental Materials

You cannot expect any single curriculum in any public school, private school, or homeschool to meet all the learning standards for the grade level and subject area in your state. Many will meet 90 percent of the standards, and some will meet 75 percent, which is why there are supplemental materials. Schools use them, and so should you. They are simply extra materials that help your child learn more. Examples of these materials include:

- *Trade books.* These are just books that are not textbooks or workbooks—in other words, they're the kinds of books, fiction and nonfiction, that you would check out at the library or that your child would choose at a bookstore. Trade books don't have to tell about many things in a limited number of pages, so they can tell a lot more about a single topic than a textbook can. They give your child a chance to practice skills that he or she is learning. If you choose wisely, you can find books that enhance reading readiness skills, such as retelling based on pictures, repetitive text, and rhyming. Sometimes these skills will be set in the context of newly learned social studies or science topics, such as real or make-believe animals; snowy, rainy, or sunny days; or families. Many companies provide these types of books for sale, but the most recognizable one may be Scholastic, Inc. Appendix A lists some books that are really good for preschoolers.

- *Software and the Internet.* Schools choose electronic activities and content, such as educational software and Internet sites, and electronic components, such as Leapfrog's LeapMat, allowing your child to expand his content knowledge while implementing skills just learned. Supplementing what your child is learning at school with these resources helps him gain technology skills within a familiar context. If you choose wisely, such as by starting with the software choices listed in appendix B of this book, you can sometimes enhance pre-reading skills and/or supplement a social studies or science topic while your child learns to operate a computer—talk about bang for your buck.

- *Other materials.* Videos, photographs, audio recordings—just about anything you can find that helps expand what your child is learning is a supplemental resource. Loosely defined, supplemental resources can include a wide array of materials; your newly trained eye is limited only to what you know is appropriate for your child.

Now you know what we need to cover, so let's get to it.

Preschool Development

2

The journey begins. Good teachers base their activities on the developmental stages at which their students are performing. What is a developmental stage, and why is it important?

The ability to learn is always related to your child's stage of intellectual development. Developmental stages describe how a child thinks and learns in different growth periods. These periods are loosely defined by age but are more accurately defined by behavior. They are important because children cannot learn something until physical growth gives them certain abilities; children who are at a certain stage cannot be taught the concepts of a higher stage (Brainerd, 1978).

The theory of child development that is the basis for modern teaching was formed by Jean Piaget, who was born in 1896 in Neuchâtel, Switzerland, and died in 1980. His theories have been expanded by other educators but stand as the foundation of today's classroom.

Piaget's Stages of Cognitive Development

Piaget is best known for his stages of cognitive development. He discovered that children think and reason differently at different periods in their lives, and he believed that everyone passes through a sequence of four distinct stages in exactly the same order, but the times in which children pass through them can vary by years. Piaget also described two processes that people use from infancy through adulthood to adapt: assimilation and accommodation. *Assimilation* is the process of using the environment to place information in a category of things you know. *Accommodation* is the process of using the environment to add a new category of things you know. Both tools are implemented throughout life and can be used together to understand a new piece of information.

Okay, did you assimilate and accommodate that? The main thing Piaget tells us is that kids really can't learn certain information and skills until they reach a certain place in their growth that is determined by years and behaviors. Understanding Piaget's stages is like getting the key to Learning City because it is a behavior map that tells you what your kids are ready to learn. Let's define the stages, then look at the behaviors. Piaget's four stages of cognitive development are:

1. *Sensorimotor stage (0 to 4 years):* In this period, intelligence is demonstrated through activity without the use of symbols (letters and numbers). Knowledge of the world is limited because it is based on actual experiences or physical interactions. Physical development (mobility) allows children to cultivate new intellectual abilities. Children will start to recognize some letters and numbers toward the end of this stage.

2. *Preoperational stage (4 to 7 years):* Intelligence is demonstrated through the use of oral language as well as letters and numbers. Memory is strengthened and imagination is developed. Children don't yet think logically very often, and it is hard for them to reverse their thinking on their own. Your little angel is still pretty egocentric at this age, and that is normal.

3. *Concrete operational stage (7 to 11 years):* As children enter this stage, they begin to think logically and will start to reverse

thinking on their own—for example, they will begin to complete inverse math operations (checking addition with subtraction, etc.). Expressing themselves by writing becomes easier. Logical thinking and expression is almost always about a concrete object, not an idea. Finally, children begin to think about other people more—they realize that things happen that affect others either more or less than they affect themselves.

4. *Formal operational stage (11 years and up):* As children become formally operational, they are able to do all the things in the concrete operational stage—but this time with ideas. Children are ready to understand concepts and to study scientific theories instead of scientific discoveries. They can learn algebra and other math concepts not represented by concrete objects that can be counted. Whereas every stage until now has continuously moved forward, this is the only stage where a step back occurs. As a teenager, your child will become egocentric once again. It won't be easy for you. Thinking and acting as if the world exists exclusively for him or her is cute behavior for a four-year-old; it is rarely cute for a teenager.

Unfortunately, only 35 percent of high school graduates in industrialized countries obtain formal operations; many people will not ever think formally. However, most children can be taught formal operations.

The graph on page 18 puts the stages in a clear perspective.

Developmental Goals for Four-Year-Olds

As the parent of a potential preschooler, first ask yourself, "Is my child ready for school?" That depends on several things, including chronological age. Even if your child is on target in terms of age, however, it is important that she has also reached certain developmental milestones.

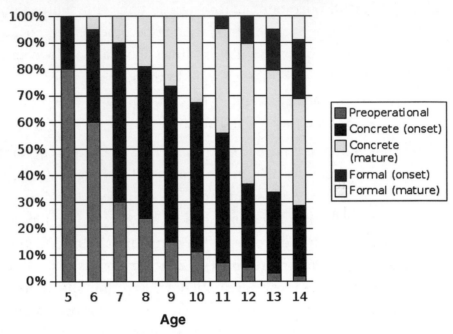

Now that you know the basics of developmental indicators, let's get down to the nitty-gritty of what can be expected from your preschooler. A four-year-old can:

- Speak fairly complex sentences ("The baby ate the cookie before I put it on the table.")

- Enjoy singing simple songs, rhymes, and nonsense words

- Learn name and phone number, and if taught may be able to print it

- Follow two unrelated directions: "Put your milk on the table and get your coat on."

- Use a spoon, fork, and dinner knife skillfully

- Dress himself or herself without much help

- Walk a straight line

- Hop on one foot

- Pedal and steer a tricycle skillfully

- Jump over objects five to six inches in height

- Place objects in a line from largest to smallest

- Recognize some letters of the alphabet, if taught

- Recognize familiar words in simple books or signs (such as a Stop sign)

- Count one to seven objects out loud

- Understand and obey simple rules (most of the time)

- Take turns and share (most of the time), but may still be bossy

- Change the rules of a game as he or she goes along

- Have difficulty separating make-believe from reality

Your child needs to achieve most of the milestones on this list to be truly ready for preschool. Developmental variances exist, but tolerance of them is more limited at this critical stage than at other stages. There is a threshold for acceptable behavior that includes physical and social maturity, focus, and cognitive structures that allow learning. A younger child is not likely to have all these attributes. If you are really struggling with deciding whether or not your child is ready to start preschool, talk to the preschool teacher whom your child is likely to have if he or she starts school this year. Many times teachers can see developmental stages more easily than parents can.

Developmental Goals for Five-Year-Olds

Some, if not most, preschoolers will turn five during the school year. Here are some things you can expect from your five-year-old. A five-year-old can:

- Verbally communicate needs, wants, and thoughts
- Use complete sentences to recount an event
- Ask questions
- Go to the bathroom by himself or herself
- Wash and dry hands
- Put on and button or zip his or her own coat
- Share and take turns when playing with other children
- Easily separate himself or herself from parents
- Approach new activities with enthusiasm and curiosity
- Follow two-step directions
- Run, hop, walk, skip, and throw a ball
- Hold crayons, pencils, and scissors properly

Now, you may be thinking, Oh no! My child is all over both lists! Remember, children vary greatly. It is common to find a two-and-a-half-year difference in development among children. Four- to five-year-olds who lag in specific skills often compensate by exceeding expectations in other areas of development. Don't worry. The best indicator of whether a child is in danger of falling behind is the rate of growth rather than an inventory of skills. If your child is making progress along the rough developmental continuum, don't be overly concerned about a few skills here and there.

Preschool Learning 3

Learning? Don't you mean playing? Isn't preschool about playing, taking naps, and having snacks? Well, sure it is, but it is about a lot more than that too. Preschool classrooms may look like a playroom— with a section set up to play house, another for art, another for playing, and the cots for naps—but there is a method to the madness. Look closer—do you see it? There are important learning and social skills being taught here. What looks like playtime is preparing your child for more formal classroom environments with a larger intake of information and skills.

A good preschool directs play activities in a way that promotes learning and helps identify the ways in which your child learns best. These are called learning styles.

Learning Styles

Learning styles define how your child learns and processes information. Education experts have identified three main types of learning: physical, visual, and auditory. When learning a new math concept, for example, a visual learner will grasp the material more quickly by reading about it in a book or watching his teacher solve a problem on the chalkboard. An auditory learner will understand the concept if she can listen to the teacher explain it and then answer questions. A physical learner (also known as tactile-kinesthetic) may need to use blocks, an abacus, or other counting materials (also known as manipulatives) to practice the new concept.

If you understand that your child is a visual learner most of the time—that is, he is most comfortable using sight to explore the world, you can play to his strength and incorporate other learning styles when appropriate. It isn't unusual to interchange learning styles for different subjects. An auditory learner can easily use kinesthetic strategies to comprehend new math concepts.

Studies have shown that accommodating a child's learning style can significantly increase his or her performance at school. In 1992, the U.S. Department of Education found that teaching to a child's learning style was one of the few strategies that improved the scores of special education students on national tests. Identifying your child's learning styles and helping him or her within that context may be the single most significant factor in your child's academic achievement. Each activity in the subject area chapters of this book lists variations that help you customize the activity to your child's learning style. Look for the symbols by the name of each learning style and use these styles to tailor the activities to your child's needs.

Learning styles are pretty easy to spot. All you have to do is watch your child's behavior when given a new piece of information.

🖐 Kinesthetic

Does your child need to touch everything? Physical learners (also known as tactile-kinesthetic learners—*tactile* for touch, *kinesthetic* for movement) use their hands or bodies to absorb new information. In some ways, everyone is a physical learner. If you peek into a classroom, you will see the physical learner tapping a pencil, finger, or foot, or twirling her hair to help her concentrate. These kids can't sit still and are in the top percentile for being diagnosed with attention deficit disorder (ADD.)

Before you run to the doctor because your child can't sit still, carefully observe him over a long period of time. Is the movement productive? Does he absorb or block information when moving? If he prefers to feel things in his hands or performs steady movement when trying to concentrate, he is engaging in productive learning.

Physical learners enjoy hands-on activities, such as cutting construction paper, sorting objects with their hands, and building (relatively) elaborate projects. When you ask physical learners to listen to a story, it is fine if she moves around while you tell it. A physical learner engages in learning more when physically engaged as well. So your child may be playing with a small toy while listening to a story. Physical learners will easily associate numbers with corresponding amounts.

👁 Visual

Would you give your right arm to get your child to listen to you? Are your walls a mural comprising every crayon your child has held? If you answered yes, you have a visual learner. You may not be able to get your child to listen to a story, but you can get him to watch the same story on a DVD or look at a book while you are reading. Your child can retell complex stories just by looking at one or two pictures from a book. Why is your child seemingly brilliant when looking at something and a space case when listening? Visual learners rely primarily on their sense of sight to take in information, understand it, and remember it. As long as they can see it, they can comprehend it.

Technically there are two kinds of visual learners: picture learners and print learners. Most children are a mixture of both, although some are one or the other (Willis and Hodson, 1999). Picture learners think in images and will easily recognize their names, the shape of the signs for their favorite restaurants, and other images. These kids like to draw—but you knew that by looking at your walls, right? Print learners think in language symbols: letters, numbers, and words—even at this age your child will be demonstrating an affinity for recognizing the shapes of written language. Print learners learn to read quickly and are good spellers right off the bat. They also like to write—even if it is play writing, that is the first step in writing!

♪ Auditory

Is your child a talker? Is total silence the kiss of death to her concentration? Auditory learners understand new ideas and concepts best when they hear and talk about the information. If you observe a group of kids, auditory learners are the ones who learn a tune in a snap just from hearing someone sing it, or who can follow directions to the letter after being told only once or twice what to do. Some auditory learners concentrate better on a task when they have music or noise in the background, or retain new information more accurately when they talk it out. Auditory learners are talkers and listeners. These kids will listen to a story and talk to you about it the entire time you try to tell it. Your child easily comprehends oral communication and actively participates in it.

Cognitive Learning

Cognitive learning levels are another way that teachers describe how a child processes information. I hear you saying, "Wow—how much of this do I have to remember?"—and you know I am going to say, "All of it," but it is really important. Let's recap for a minute to see how all of this fits together.

First, you learned about developmental stages, the physical growth that needs to happen before your child can learn certain things. Second, you learned about learning styles, the way your child prefers to process information. Third, you are about to learn about cognitive learning levels, the level at which your child knows, understands, and can use information that he or she learns.

Piaget identified the developmental stages in the 1930s and 1940s. By the 1950s, a group of researchers got together, led by Benjamin Bloom, and created the cognitive learning taxonomy designed to help you understand the levels of learning that can occur with new information. Bloom is often considered one of the most important educational theorists of the twentieth century. A professor at the University of Chicago, Bloom was more than a brilliant teacher: he was a brilliant thinker. Bloom spent his career researching how thinking and learning happen in students of all ages. Bloom and his researchers broke down the learning levels as follows:

Level 1: Knowledge. The things you know—bits of information that you can memorize, such as the ABCs.

Level 2: Comprehension. The things you understand—knowing the ABCs and understanding that they represent sounds.

Level 3: Application. The things you can apply—knowing the ABCs, understanding that they represent sounds, and then sounding out a word.

Level 4: Analysis. The things you understand well enough to think about in a new way—knowing the ABCs, understanding that they represent sounds, sounding out a word, and then figuring out what the word means.

Level 5: Synthesis. Understanding something well enough to apply it to a new situation—knowing the ABCs, understanding that they represent sounds, sounding out a word, figuring out what the word means, and using it in a new way.

Level 6: Evaluation. Understanding something so well that you can tell if it is being used correctly—knowing the ABCs, understanding that they represent sounds, sounding out a word, figuring out what the word means, using it in a new way, and figuring out if the new way was right.

Check the Bloom's Cognitive Learning Levels table on page 27 for some specific key words and behaviors for each level. Getting to know the key words will help you determine how to ask your child questions in order to find out the level at which she understands new information. While most preschoolers will be in the knowledge, comprehension, and application levels, it is important to identify which of these levels your child is operating at so that you can manage your expectations of your child appropriately. Use the examples in the right-hand column of the table to ask questions that check for each level of understanding.

Bloom's Cognitive Learning Levels

Cognitive Level	Verb	Key Words		Examples
Knowledge Recalls data. Exhibits memory of previously learned material by recalling facts and basic concepts.	Remember	choose define describe find how identify know label list match name omit outline recall	recognize reproduce select show spell state tell what when where which who why	• Defines terminology/vocabulary • Describes details and elements • Recognizes classifications and categories • Knows principles, generalizations, theories, models, and structures • Knows subject-specific skills, algorithms, techniques, and methods • Names criteria for using certain procedures • Spells words • Outlines facts, events, stories, or ideas
Comprehension Demonstrates understanding of facts and ideas by organizing, comparing, translating, interpreting, giving descriptions, and stating main ideas. Understands the meaning, translation, interpolation, and interpretation of instructions and problems.	Understand	classify compare comprehend contrast convert defend demonstrate distinguish estimate explain extend illustrate	infer interpret outline paraphrase predict relate rephrase rewrite show summarize translate	• Summarizes or retells information • Translates an equation • Outlines the main ideas • Summarizes instructions, facts, details, or other things • Compares and contrasts ideas • Explains what is happening • Identifies statements to support a conclusion • Classifies information

(continued)

Bloom's Cognitive Learning Levels *(continued)*

Cognitive Level	Verb	Key Words		Examples
Application Solves problems in new situations by applying acquired knowledge, facts, techniques, and rules in a different way. Uses a concept in a new situation or unprompted use of an abstraction. Applies what was learned in the classroom into novel situations.	Apply	apply build change choose compute construct demonstrate develop discover identify interview manipulate	model modify operate plan predict prepare produce relate select show solve utilize	• Applies a formula to solve a problem • Uses a manual to solve a problem • Describes how to use something • Finds examples to help apply ideas, rules, steps, or an order • Describes a result • Modifies ideas, rules, steps, or an order for use in another way • Selects facts to demonstrate something
Analysis Examines and breaks information into parts by identifying motives or causes. Makes inferences and finds evidence to support generalizations. Separates material or concepts into component parts so that its organizational structure may be understood. Distinguishes between facts and inferences.	Analyze	analyze assume categorize classify compare conclusion contrast discover dissect distinction distinguish	divide examine function inference inspect list motive relationships take part in test for theme	• Troubleshoots a problem using logical deduction • Lists components or parts of a whole • Names the function of something • Makes a distinction between two or more things • Classifies or categorizes a number of things • Draws a conclusion • Lists the parts of a whole

Bloom's Cognitive Learning Levels *(continued)*

Cognitive Level	Verb	Key Words		Examples
Synthesis				
Compiles information in a different way by combining elements in a new pattern or proposing alternative solutions. Builds a structure or pattern from diverse elements. Puts parts together to form a whole, with emphasis on creating a new meaning or structure.	Create	adapt arrange build categorize change choose combine compile compose construct create delete design develop devise discuss elaborate estimate explain formulate generate happen imagine improve	invent make up maximize minimize modify organize original originate plan predict propose rearrange reconstruct relate reorganize revise rewrite solution solve summarize suppose tell test write	• Integrates training from several sources to solve a problem • Formulates a theory • Invents a solution • Constructs a model • Compiles facts • Minimizes or maximizes an event or item • Designs a solution, model, or project • Adapts something to create another thing
Evaluation				
Presents and defends opinions by making judgments about information, validity of ideas, or quality of work based on a set of criteria.	Evaluate	agree appraise assess award choose compare conclude criteria	importance influence interpret judge justify mark measure opinion	• Selects the most effective solution • Explains a selection, conclusion, or recommendation • Prioritizes facts • Rates or ranks facts, characters (people), or events • Assesses the value or importance of something

(continued)

Bloom's Cognitive Learning Levels *(continued)*

Cognitive Level	Verb	Key Words		Examples
Evaluation (continued) Makes judgments about the value of ideas or materials.		criticize decide deduct defend determine disprove dispute estimate evaluate explain	perceive prioritize prove rank rate recommend rule on select support value	• Justifies a selection, conclusion, or recommendation

Source: Adapted from Benjamin S. Bloom, *Taxonomy of Educational Objectives: The Classification of Educational Goals, by a Committee of College and University Examiners* (New York: Longmans, Green, 1956).

The Standards   4

Standards-based education came into the national spotlight well over a decade ago. Standards were implemented slowly in all subjects and grades, and now the majority of states even have preschool learning standards. The idea behind the standards reform movement is straightforward: when states set clear standards defining what a child should know and be able to do in certain grades, teachers and learners are able to focus their efforts and highlight particular areas in which they need improvement. Ideally, the standards show teachers what they need to teach, by allowing curricula and (informal) assessments that measure performance to be aligned with the standards.

As with all reform movements, there are people who disagree with the idea of creating common learning standards—whether it is for preschool or high school. They primarily point to tendencies to simply "teach the test" and complain that the standards limit content breadth and community input. Since there is no real test to teach a preschooler, it makes sense that the real gripe may lie in the fact that education has always been a local issue. It is easy to fear change when you fear that community values may be lost by standardizing state curriculum. Others believe that standards even the playing field. Before you form your own opinion, let's take a look at standards-based education.

Standards-based education lists content and skills that children need to learn at each grade level. Success depends on combining content and performance standards with consistent curriculum and instruction as well as appropriate assessment and accountability. This is the point where teachers and learners start to feel anxious. Everything sounds very official, particularly the accountability part. What does this language mean, and what happens if children don't meet the learning standards requirements?

Relax—there are no learning standards police patrolling our neighborhood schools, libraries, and bookstores. There are simply baselines by which the state determines eligibility for a high school diploma.

Let's start by defining learning standards.

Types of Learning Standards

Learning standards are broad statements that describe what content a child should know and what skills a child should be able to do in different subject areas.

Content standards are a form of learning standards that describe the topics to be studied, not the skills to be performed.

Performance standards are a form of learning standards that describe the skills to be performed, not the content to be studied.

Public school teachers must ensure that their students are taught the required content and skills because they are accountable not only to the students but also to their state, their school district, and their community for every child's performance on test scores. Private schools are accountable to their constituency with respect to student performance, but they are not accountable to the public. In fact, school requirements as well as teacher licensure are not as strictly monitored for private schools. The academically strong private schools institute internal standards that meet or exceed state expectations for public schools, but there are private schools that feel that other aspects of child development, such as religious development, take precedence over academics. If your child attends private school, you must research the school to make sure it meets your expectations both academically and socially.

For preschool education, "early learning standards" spell out the expectations for the learning and development of young children (National Association for the Education of Young Children and National Association of Early Childhood Specialists in State Departments of Education, 2002).

The use of testing to monitor classroom instruction is central to the theory of standards-based reform. Preschool is a little early to sit a child down and ask him to take a test showing us what he knows—particularly considering that preschoolers still need help reading and writing—so preschool assessment more often uses informal assessment, which relies primarily on observation. The main purpose of setting preschool standards is to make the learning and development expectations uniform across the fifty states. Setting standards also helps preschools target which educational materials or activities will best help children achieve a certain proficiency level before entering kindergarten. While it seems odd to set learning standards for kids who aren't old enough to start reading yet, there are certain things that children need to be able to do before they can read, write, or do math. In that light, preschool learning standards start to make sense.

Learning Standards Resources

Each state has created a document that describes what children are supposed to know about and what they are supposed to be able to do at each grade level and in each subject area. You may wonder who writes the standards and why you should believe that these people know what is best. A lot of public school teachers have wondered the same thing.

You can rest assured that writing the state learning standards is a collaborative effort. Most states rely on input from experts who know about the grade level and subject area. These experts can include teachers, researchers, people from the education industry, and school administrators. In an endnote or a footnote, each document lists the people hired by the state to help write the final version.

You can locate the standards that apply to your child through your State Department of Education's Web site, by calling your State Department of Education, or through the Internet at www. knowledgeessentials.com. There are several things you should read for:

1. *Content standards:* What topics will your child be studying?

2. *Performance standards:* What skills must your child develop by the end of the year?

3. *Resources:* What resources are designed to help teachers meet the learning standards? Can you access them?

4. *Correlation reports:* Does the state provide a listing of how the required textbooks and other materials meet their own learning standards? Your school district should also be able to provide you with this information.

As you read your state's learning standards document, you may notice that you don't always agree with what is listed for your child to be learning. Is there anything you can do?

If your child attends a public school, there is little you can do to protest the prescribed curricula, but you can certainly enhance the curricula through learning activities at home. If your child attends a private school, you may have greater influence over classroom activities (as a paying customer), but you will probably not get the curricula changed to meet your concerns.

If you teach your child at home, then you have as much control as you would like over your child's curricula. You undoubtedly have specific beliefs that have led you to decide to homeschool, and you can remain true to those beliefs while still covering the required curricula. Even if you don't believe the required curricula are entirely appropriate, the assessments required by the states and higher education institutions will be normed to the learning standards of the state in which you live. The standards are just the basics that your child will need to succeed in mainstream society. There are many more opportunities for learning across a wide range of subjects that can be totally up to you.

Preschool Reading Readiness

5

Helping your child get ready to read isn't as cut-and-dried as, say, getting him ready to play in the snow. There's no special suit or fancy equipment. Reading is about communicating. Sure there are letters to learn and rules to follow, but when you get down to basics, you are communicating. You are your child's role model, so it's important to pay attention to your communication skills when interacting with your child.

Talk with your children. Such everyday activities as eating lunch, cleaning up toys, or taking a bath provide opportunities to talk and to listen. Here are some tips on what you can do to help your child develop reading readiness skills:

> ## Beginning of Preschool Reading Readiness Checklist
>
> Students who are working at the standard level at the beginning of preschool:
>
> ____ Can tell their own name to others
>
> ____ Enjoy lullabies and nursery rhymes
>
> ____ Enjoy finger plays
>
> ____ Can retell events from a familiar story
>
> ____ Ask questions
>
> ____ Are curious
>
> ____ Begin to know the difference between pretend and real
>
> ____ Can identify some reasons for happiness, sadness, or anger

- Be an active listener. Stop what you are doing when your child talks to you, look at her, and respond with comments that are relevant. Listening and responding to a child is the best way to discover how she thinks and learns. Listening also shows your child that she is communicating her feelings and ideas.

- Don't underestimate the value of play! Playing allows children to mimic what they see older kids and adults doing. You will see your child play-read, play-write, play school, play-play-play. As your child explores, gets creative, and develops social skills, he is also developing communication skills that are essential to reading.

- Read together daily. Fostering your child's love of books is a gift that will last a lifetime!

- Talking about experiences, telling a story, and sharing a picture book are central to emergent literacy. Expose your four-year-old to many language and reading experiences that are fun and playful, including nursery rhymes, rhyming games, singing, and lap and bedtime reading. Your child will enjoy hearing books about things that are familiar; this helps her connect to the story. Four-year-olds usually like picture books with just a few words on the page, and books that use repetition or predictable print. Your child will probably want to say the words with you as you read.

Developmentally, four-year-olds usually have a short attention span. Follow your child's lead and continue only as long as he is happy. Keeping activities fun and playful is very important at this stage; this is not the time for drills and teaching materials.

Words Have Meaning

Does your little one scribble a big mess of lines and then ask you to read it? You may not be able to decipher it, but this scribble is a good sign. Your child is beginning to be aware that words are written and have meanings. He is showing you that he knows that written things have meaning, but he hasn't yet started to recognize letters and that letters make up words.

Recognizing environmental print is another important milestone in realizing that words have meaning. The word that most children recognize first is their own name because they usually see it most often. Your child will recognize signs of stores or products that she likes because the signs are easier to "read." Those big yellow arches are pure genius when it comes to name recognition in the pre-reading set.

Letter-Sound Relationships

Each letter in the alphabet has a name and at least one sound. Knowing that letters have sounds is different from saying the alphabet or naming the letter when it is shown to you. Understanding letter-sound relationships is seeing a letter and connecting it to the sound that the letter makes. This is an important step in the reading process, especially sounding out or blending sounds to make words.

Letter-Sound Relationship Skills	Having Problems?	Quick Tips
Can segment the sounds in words	Doesn't seem to recognize the letters in words	Your child needs to watch you write words. Begin by saying all the sounds in the word and saying the names of the letters that make the sounds as you write them. Do the same when your child dictates words for you to write. The ability to do this is important in spelling.
Can match words that begin with the same sound	Doesn't discriminate beginning sounds of words	Shower your child with oral language. Talk, sing, play rhyming games, and read books at every opportunity. Listen when your child talks, and stop what you are doing to look at her.
Recognizes own name	Scribbles, then wants me to read it	Write the words that your child dictates to you, preferably at his eye level. Explain that letters put together make words. Think aloud as you model writing words. Segment the sounds of the word and then say the letters that make the sounds as you write them.

Letter-Sound Relationships Activities

 ## 1 Letter Recognition

TIME: 15 minutes

MATERIALS
- cardboard or construction paper
- safety scissors
- glue
- old magazines and catalogues

Using the first letter of your child's first name, cut out a large (12 × 18) letter shape from the cardboard or construction paper.

Learning happens when: you sit with your child, look through the magazines and catalogues, and locate pictures of things that begin with the same letter sound as his first name. Cut out the pictures and glue them onto the cardboard letter to make a letter collage. "Read" the pictures with your child, emphasizing the beginning sound of each word.

Variations: Use copies of photos of your child; make the collage more personal by making a photo letter collage. Cover the collage with clear contact paper and hang it on the wall.

For your kinesthetic learner, add some movement to this activity by asking him to help gather materials. Discuss the project and ask your child to retell the directions. He will want to turn the pages of the magazines to find pictures for the collage. Instead of making a paper letter, ask your child to make the letter with his body while lying on the floor. Outline the letter using masking tape.

Ask your visual learner to describe details of the pictures in the collage using various attributes. For example, he may identify the color by saying, "This is a red dress." He might also use two attributes and say, "This is a pretty red dress."

With your auditory learner, say a rhyme, sing a song, or say a tongue twister that uses the sound of the first letter in his own name. This will help familiarize your child with this letter before beginning the project. Be sure to "read" the finished product aloud with your child. Check out these resources for rhymes and songs:

Internet Sites

www.preschoolrainbow.org/preschool-rhymes.htm

http://www.falcon.jmu.edu/~ramseyil/fingerplayindex.htm

www.kididdles.com/mouseum/busy.html

Books

1001 Rhymes and Fingerplays (paperback), by Totline (compiler); Totline Publications, 1994

Little Hands, Fingerplays and Action Songs: Seasonal Activities and Creative Play for 2- to 6-Year-Olds (Williamson Little Hands Series, paperback), by Emily Stetson, Vicky Congdon, and Betsy Day (illustrator); Williamson Publishing, 2001

Musical Games, Fingerplays and Rhythmic Activities for Early Childhood (paperback), by Marian Wirth et al.; Prentice Hall, 1993

You can find more links to finger plays, rhymes, and songs at www.knowledgeessentials.com.

Mastery occurs when: your child can tell you the first letter of his name and can tell you whether a word begins with the sound of that letter.

You may want to help your child a little more if: he has trouble recognizing the sounds. Sit with your child and exaggerate the beginning sounds by saying the name of each picture and repeating his name. Immediately correct any errors without judgment. (For example, if your child chooses a picture that doesn't have the same letter as his name, say "This one starts with 'duh' and your name starts with 'sss'.") If using scissors is hard for your child, try alternating by cutting one picture and tearing the next one.

2 Guessing Game

Time: 20 minutes

MATERIALS
- large paper bag
- marker
- small objects and toys that begin with the same letter
- blindfold
- unlined paper

Learning happens when: your child identifies hidden objects. Place the small objects and toys into the bags and blindfold your child. Hold the bag and ask your child to reach in and pick up one object. She should feel the object and guess what it is. Say the names of the toys, emphasizing the beginning sound, and tell your child the letter that makes the sound. Look around with her to find other things that begin with the same sound to put into the bag. Repeat the activity; this time, see if your child can name the objects and the beginning sound. Continue until she tires of the activity. Then, using a marker, draw that letter on unlined paper and indicate the starting point and the steps involved in drawing the letter. Make another one using dots that your child can connect to make the letter. Give your child a marker and ask her to make the letter on her own.

Variations: After completing the main activity, read a storybook to your child and take notice of all the words that begin with the same sound.

- After completing the main activity, ask your kinesthetic learner to put away the collected objects.

- After completing the main activity, ask your visual learner to put the objects in order from smallest to largest.

- After completing the main activity, ask your auditory learner to name all the objects, emphasize the sound of the beginning letter, and identify the letter name.

Mastery occurs when: your child can tell you the name of the letter and the sound it makes.

You may want to help your child a little more if: she gets tired of playing. Don't force her to complete it. Put it away and come back to it later. It should be a fun activity approached as a game.

3 | Letter Play

Pick a letter for this activity and cut out ten of the same letter shapes from the index cards.

Learning happens when: you read the book to your child as he looks for the selected letter on each page. After reading, review the letter sound. Go into your child's room and have him look for objects that also start with that sound, and continue in other rooms as needed. Each time your child discovers something that matches the sound of the letter, tape a letter to it. Try to find ten objects.

Variations: Take a walk with your child and look for objects that begin with the correct sound.

🖐 Ask your kinesthetic learner to use modeling clay to sculpt something and tell you the object's name and the beginning sound of the name.

👁 Ask your visual learner to do letter rubbings using a cardboard cutout of the letter, white paper, and an old crayon with the paper torn off. Have your child place the cutout under the paper, turn the crayon on its side, and rub the crayon over the cutout. He may want to do this again using other colors.

👂 Sing the alphabet song with your auditory learner. Say a letter and ask him to name something that begins with that sound.

TIME: 10 minutes

MATERIALS
▪ alphabet book (for example, *Chicka Chicka Boom Boom,* by Bill Martin Jr.)
▪ index cards
▪ tape

Mastery occurs when: your child recognizes the letter chosen for the activity and can tell you the sound it makes.

You may want to help your child a little more if: he can't discriminate between the beginning sound and ending sound. Stress the sound as you say a word. Try saying two words while stressing the beginning sounds and ask if they begin the same way. Give immediate feedback, but don't dwell on it or say "No, that's wrong" if he makes mistakes. Say something like "Your name starts with ___ [insert sound], and this word begins with ___ [insert sound]."

4 Beginning Sounds

TIME: 10 minutes

MATERIALS
- coloring book
- crayons
- unlined paper

Learning happens when: your child colors pictures in a coloring book as you talk about the name of the object she is coloring and the sound of its first letter. Let your child choose the page to color. Help her color the pictures if necessary. Then model writing that letter for your child. If she is interested in trying to write the letter, spend some time doing this. Continue only as long as your child is interested.

Variations: Read an alphabet book to your child, such as *ABC,* by Dr. Seuss. Make a poster of pictures that begin with any letter that your child chooses; let her look at the book to find a letter if necessary. Use pictures from old magazines or coloring books to make the poster. You'll need glue, scissors, and unlined paper to do this activity.

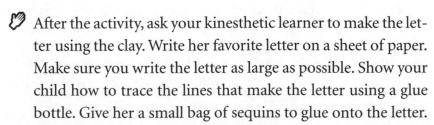 After the activity, ask your kinesthetic learner to make the letter using the clay. Write her favorite letter on a sheet of paper. Make sure you write the letter as large as possible. Show your child how to trace the lines that make the letter using a glue bottle. Give her a small bag of sequins to glue onto the letter.

👁 For your visual learner, draw a tree trunk and let your child use letter stamps and a stamp pad to match the letters from the book as they are introduced in the story. Label the work. See how many letters your child can name.

👂 For your auditory learner, sing a short song that your child really likes—it can be about anything. Pick a word from the song and say it, stressing the beginning sound; ask your child to name another word that starts the same way.

Mastery occurs when: Your child can match letters to their corresponding sounds. Your child can identify beginning sounds in words that you say aloud.

You may want to help your child a little more if: she cannot identify beginning sounds. Repeat some of the earlier activities. Continue to point out letters at every opportunity. Label photos with names of the objects and post them at eye level.

5 | Memory Game

Learning happens when: you and your child play by the rules of the Memory Game, modified to make it easier and quicker. Choose eight cards and make sure that you have matching pairs. When a match is found, say the beginning sound of the pictured word and write the letter.

Variations: Use the Memory Game cards to sort pictures into two categories: pictures that start with the same sound as your child's name and pictures that don't. Make Memory Game cards that have letters on them and play the game to look for matching letters.

TIME: 10 minutes

MATERIALS
- Memory Game
- paper
- marker

✍ For your kinesthetic learner, draw the letter that his name begins with on construction paper or cardboard; show him how to trace the letter using glue, and glue on something that begins with that letter—for example, for Carl, glue cotton balls onto a C; for Ella, glue broken eggshells onto an E; for Nancy, glue nuts onto an N.

👁 When playing the Memory Game with your visual learner, ask him to point to the beginning letter on an alphabet strip every time he gets a match.

👂 Teach your auditory learner the Name Game song. (Andy! Andy, Andy, bo bandy bonana fanna fo fandy, fee fy mo mandy, Andy!) Later, sing the song using your child's name and the names of other people in your family. Ask him to name the pictures on the Memory cards and tell you which ones begin with the beginning sound of his first name.

Mastery occurs when: your child recognizes the beginning sounds of words and makes some letter matches to the sound.

You may want to help your child a little more if: he is still having problems remembering the letters. Encourage your child. Continue to practice the fun activities introduced so far, talk about letters, and point out your child's name on a regular basis. This is a difficult skill, but one that can be mastered with practice.

6 | Labeling

Use index cards and write out the names of many things your child sees and uses everyday. Write one word on each card and laminate it. Make a card for the door, mirror, bed, toys, sink, tub, and so on.

Learning happens when: your child labels everything! This activity will help with word and letter association and with building confidence in beginning to "read." Read each card with your child, go through the house together, and ask her to tape the cards to the corresponding objects. Help her as needed. When reading each card, stress the initial sound of the word and point to the letter that makes the sound.

Variations: For a more challenging variation, write the labels, show them to your child, and read each word while stressing the initial sound. See if your child can pick out the label whose word starts with that sound. This is the beginning of using initial consonant clues to identify unknown words.

   Ask your kinesthetic learner to find five other objects that she would like to have you label. Write the labels while she is watching; as you write, say the name of each letter that you write. Have your child attach the labels to the objects. You can use a timer for this activity for a little excitement.

   Let your visual learner "write" some labels. She will probably be the only person who knows what she wrote, so ask her to "read" them to you. It is normal for visual learners to want to write, and you can probably tell what she is trying to write by following her line of vision to the object she is thinking about. If you are sure enough of what your child is "writing" on the label, you can offer to "read" it to her.

   Go on a "reading" walk with your auditory learner. Walk through the house and ask her to "read" the labels that you put up earlier.

Mastery occurs when: your child notices the words and attempts to "read" them.

TIME: 10 minutes

MATERIALS
- index cards
- markers
- clear contact paper
- tape

You may want to help your child a little more if: she thinks this is a hard activity. Point out that the object is represented by the word on the card. Be sure to stress the initial sound and point to the letter that makes the sound. Repeat some of the earlier activities or their variations.

7 Letter Cards

TIME: 10 minutes

MATERIALS
■ 26 index cards
■ markers

Write one letter of the alphabet on each index card.

Learning happens when: you place five of the index cards in front of your child so that he can see them, say the name of an object, and have your child choose the letter that the object begins with. Continue the activity with the other letter cards.

Variations: Teach your child a favorite song that repeats words with the same beginning sounds. (Raffi has several tunes that work well, such as "Baby Beluga." Another good song for this activity is "Really Rosie," by Carole King.) Talk about the letter that makes the sound. Prepare a sheet of coloring pictures that begin with that sound. Talk with your child about each picture and the beginning sound, then ask him to draw a ring around the whole picture if it begins with that sound. Be sure to exaggerate the beginning sounds as you name the pictures.

- For your kinesthetic learner, make sure that the object you name is located in your house; ask your child to identify the letter it begins with, find the object, and place the index card beside the object.

- For your visual learner, hold up an object and have him identify the letter it begins with by showing you the card with the correct letter.

👂 Auditory learners will enjoy the main activity as described.

Mastery occurs when: your child can link most letters of the alphabet with the corresponding initial letter.

You may want to help your child a little more if: he can't identify the beginning letters of objects for most of the alphabet. Reduce the number of cards to five and work on those until he has mastered them, then add several more letters.

8 | Shopping for Sounds

Make a list of the alphabet, with space between the letters so that you can add the items you find that begin with each letter.

TIME: 15 minutes

MATERIALS
▪ food items
▪ toys
▪ list of the alphabet

Learning happens when: you take your child to a store that has toys as well as food items. As you go through the store, have your child identify an item she would want to buy. When she has chosen one, ask her what letter the word begins with and then write that object beside the appropriate letter on the list. Repeat the procedure.

Variations: Sit in your child's room and play a game called What's My Sound? Ask your child to touch something in the room that begins with the same sound as "bottle," for example, as you hold the letter that makes the beginning sound. Repeat with other letters as long as the game holds your child's interest.

✋ Your kinesthetic learner will enjoy the main activity as described.

👁 For your visual learner, line up several items. Say a letter and the corresponding sound and have your child point to or pick up the item that has that beginning sound.

❁ Tell your auditory learner a letter of the alphabet. Have her repeat the name of the letter and its sound and then try to find an object that begins with that letter.

Mastery occurs when: your child can link most letters of the alphabet to objects with the corresponding initial letter.

You may want to help your child a little more if: she can't find objects to go with the letters. Stay in one aisle of the store or give hints as to what objects on that aisle begin with that letter.

Visual Comprehension

In order to read, you have to be able to understand and attach meaning to what you see. You might hear your child's teacher talk about "visual discrimination" and "visual comprehension." *Visual discrimination* means that your child can see differences and similarities between things and point them out or describe them to you. This is important because it will lead to the skill of discriminating words in print. Visual discrimination activities for preschool include working puzzles or matching one half of a picture to its other half. *Visual comprehension* means your child attaches meaning to illustrations, photographs, and pictures. Visual comprehension skills help your child retell the events of the story, make predictions about what will happen next in a story, and begin to use illustrations to clarify and comprehend the story. Your child can begin to identify feelings by looking at the illustrations.

Visual Comprehension Skills	Having Problems?	Quick Tips
Identifies businesses using their signs or logos	Doesn't seem to notice signs	Point out signs and logos to your child when you are together. You can find examples everywhere: shopping bags, packages, cereal boxes, store fronts.
Starts to recognize public and municipal signs, such as signs for men's or women's restrooms	Takes in the whole picture but doesn't notice specific signs to help him find his way	During your next outing with your child, point out signs that are important and talk with him about their meanings. Examples of signs include No Swimming, Exit, Stay off the Grass, Restrooms, and Poison.
Uses written language to identify belongings	Does not recognize her own name when it is written	Label your child's belongings and explain that this is the way she can tell for sure that these belong to her. Using cardboard, markers, and glitter, make name plates and signs with your child. Hang one on her bedroom door and on other possessions around the house.
Understands gestures	Doesn't clue in to quiet gestures	Practice specific gestures with your child and discuss their meanings. Do it as a short game (examples: putting finger to lips for "quiet," waving a greeting, motioning him to move closer).
Uses graphic cues	Starts at the back of the book	Point out book titles as you read stories to your child.
Visually discriminates shapes and spaces	Doesn't yet know the names of the basic two-dimensional shapes	Play with puzzles, mazes, and blocks.
Uses pictures and illustrations	Asks me questions about the pictures instead of giving her opinion	Ask your child specific questions about pictures. Check out the "emergent reader" books from the public library; the pictures tell the story.

Visual Comprehension Activities

1 Photo Album

TIME: 10 minutes

MATERIALS
- photos of your child
- small photo album
- markers

Select a dozen pictures of your child and arrange them in a small photo album.

Learning happens when: your child looks at the photos and talks to you about each one. Ask him to tell you about each picture and to try to recall the feelings about the time when the picture was taken. Write his words on the bottom of each corresponding photo page. Give the photo book to your child and have him "read" the book with you. Leave this book someplace where your child can go back to it often.

Variations: Place pictures of family members in a small photo album. Ask your child to name each person and tell you about him or her. Write his words on the bottom of each page.

✋ Ask your kinesthetic learner to use his toys to re-create the scenes in each picture. For instance, if you have a picture of a birthday party, you could suggest that your child set up a birthday party for his stuffed animals. If the pictures involve a cookout, ask your child to set up the people while you fix a cookout-style snack or lunch.

👁 For your visual learner, gather a large selection of pictures and let him pick out the ones that he likes best. Use these pictures in the album to make the book for the activity.

👂 Ask your auditory learner to tell you what you did to make the book in the order in which you did each step.

Mastery occurs when: your child attempts to "read" the book alone. Many people don't realize that looking at the pictures and loosely retelling the story is a pre-reading skill. The child is beginning to use picture clues and to realize that the writing represents words.

You may want to help your child a little more if: he complains that the activity is hard. Help by retelling the events surrounding the picture. Try this activity another time and let your child retell the story with his words.

2 Recalling Details

Learning happens when: you and your child watch a TV program about animals to learn new things. Ask your child to tell you what she knows about the animal before you begin to watch the program together. Make a list of the things your child tells you. Tell your child that as she watches this program, she should try to remember new things she learns about the animal. When she hears something new, ask her to tell you and write it down. After the program, read the list of new things together. Compare the lists of old facts and new facts and talk about how much more your child knows now. This is a great activity to encourage your child to talk about quality TV programs and to extend the learning from the program by talking and doing related activities. Ask your child to draw a picture showing something that she learned from the program.

Variations: Work puzzles with your child by comparing the shapes of the pieces that are needed as well as by matching colors. Ask your child to choose things in her room that look the same and other things that look different. Ask her to name feelings by "reading" the facial expressions in a book or in photos.

TIME: 40 minutes

MATERIALS
- TV program about animals
- three sheets of paper
- pencil
- crayons
- markers

You can work on visual skills by discussing the illustrations when you read a book; this teaches your child to look for picture clues to help understand the meaning of the book. You can also try working with your child to sort letters into groups of letters that are the same. You'll need multiple copies of letters of the alphabet (for example, five Bs and one each of L, H, K, M, and E could be the first group). Tell your child to sort the letters into two groups: one group of letters that are the same and another group of those that are different.

- Give your kinesthetic learner a model of the animal from the TV program. Ask her to act out the part she enjoyed most.

- Ask your visual learner to tell you when she hears new words from a program on video. Stop the video and write the word on a piece of paper as you tell your child the meaning. Later come back to the list and discuss word meaning. Let your child draw a picture that will help her remember the meaning.

- Ask your auditory learner comprehension questions that will guide her through different sequential parts of the program. Ask her to tell you what happened first, in the middle, and at the end of the video.

Mastery occurs when: your child can retell a brief sequence of the events of the story.

You may want to help your child more if: she has problems recalling details from the story after the first time you watched the program. Discuss the key scenes before you start a second viewing.

3 Self-Portrait

Learning happens when: your child draws a picture of himself looking just the way he looks today. (The clothes should have the same patterns, the hairstyle and shoes should be the same, and so on.) Roll out enough paper for your child to lie on, and trace around him using a crayon or marker. Be careful not to punch holes in the paper. Ask your child to draw inside the outline to make a self-portrait. Encourage him to notice details, such as hair and eye color, freckles, dimples, and so on. The more visual detail your child adds to the self-portrait, the greater visual discrimination and comprehension he is applying to the activity.

Variations: Use a blank paper-doll cutout instead of a large outline of your child.

TIME. 20 minutes

MATERIALS
▪ large roll of paper (brown wrapping paper or the white side of any wrapping paper works well)
▪ crayons or markers

Your kinesthetic learner should use collage materials to complete the self-portrait. You might include such items as yarn for hair, real buttons, wallpaper scraps, construction paper, sequins, and stickers.

Ask your visual learner to use a mirror as a reference for completing the self-portrait. Talk about how the details in the portrait should be the same as what he sees in the mirror.

Ask your auditory learner to repeat the directions to you before beginning and to explain what he made as you view the finished portrait. Ask questions about details to encourage an active discussion.

Mastery occurs when: your child draws a self-portrait that resembles what he looks like today. He should use colors that correspond to the colors he is wearing at the time, and such details as eyes, nose, mouth, and hair should be fairly accurate. More mature children will add ears.

You may want to help your child a little more if: he overlooks some important detail (for example, the eyes or clothes) in completing the self-portrait.

4 Rainbow Sheet

TIME: 10 minutes

MATERIALS
- old white sheet
- 2 or 3 primary food colors
- spray bottles
- water

Add water to the spray bottles and then add several drops of the food coloring until the water is tinted with the color. Gently shake the bottles to mix.

Learning happens when: your child sprays different colors onto the sheet, causing them to mix and blend. She should be able to describe the process and the changes in the sheet. You'll hear her say things about the ways the color moves and the way the color changes as another touches it.

Variations: You can use a T-shirt instead of a sheet to do the same activity. You can also use watercolors and a brush on white paper.

✋ Ask your kinesthetic learner to help you mix the food coloring and water together. What happens to the food coloring when you add it to the water? Can you make the colored water darker? What happens when you add a different color to the same water?

👁 Visual learners will be good at making different shades of the same color in their water bottles. Ask your child to keep track of the shade by counting the number of drops of food coloring used in each bottle. What happens when you spray the sheet with different shades of the same color?

👂 Let your auditory learner listen to or sing a song about colors while she works. These learners will describe the changes they observe.

Mastery occurs when: your child is able to express her observations of the changes in color that occur.

You may want to help your child a little more if: she has problems describing the changes that occurred. You should talk through the process with her as she repeats the exercise. Ask your child specific questions, such as "What happens when you spray blue on yellow? Let's try it."

5 I Draw, You Draw

Before beginning the activity, make a shape poster; include a triangle, square, rectangle, and circle.

TIME: 15 minutes

MATERIALS
▪ unlined paper
▪ markers or crayons

Learning happens when: your child draws to complete shapes that you begin. Choose a shape, name it, and point to it on the poster. Explain to your child that you will draw half the shape and he will draw the other half. Ask him to watch as you draw. When you have drawn half the shape, hand the marker to your child so that he can draw. Restate the name of the shape. After he has completed his half, explain symmetry and how it relates to the activity you just did. Using the procedure described, draw an oval and begin to draw a face: draw one ear, one eye, half a nose, half a mouth, and half a head of hair. After you draw each item, stop and wait for your child to draw one on the other side.

Variations: Play a game of Concentration using the shapes from the activities. You'll need to make doubles in order to form pairs. When a player gets a match, he or she needs to name the shape.

✋ Ask your kinesthetic learner to sit with you and play with blocks. Build something and ask your child to build the same thing. Build towers, walls, squares, pillars, or anything else that you can make with blocks; the goal is to end up with two things that are exactly alike.

👁 Your visual learner should do well at this activity. Use the opportunity to talk about butterflies and their symmetry. Print out a copy of a butterfly at www.knowledgeessentials. com and ask your child to color it symmetrically.

👂 Ask your auditory learner to retell in sequence the experience of drawing with you. Then ask your child to talk to you about what he drew and why he drew it.

Mastery occurs when: your child begins to match both sides or recognize symmetry.

You may want to help your child a little more if: he doesn't see symmetry. Place a sheet of construction paper (you can't see through it) over half of a simple picture (for example, of a tree, a house, or the sun) in a coloring book and take turns adding something to the construction paper side in order to create symmetry.

6 Letter Match

TIME: 15 minutes

MATERIALS

▪ paper
▪ crayons or markers
▪ poker chips, checkers, buttons, or similar objects

Draw a Bingo grid with nine spaces total on a sheet of paper, put a letter in each space, then write on individual smaller pieces of paper each of the letters that you used.

Learning happens when: your child plays letter-match Bingo. Hold an individual letter card where your child can easily see it; when she finds the matching letter on her Bingo card, she covers the Bingo card with the letter card. You may have to help her read the winning letters.

🖐 Kinesthetic learners should use the letter pieces from a wooden alphabet puzzle or plastic magnetic letter markers to cover up the letter called on the Bingo card.

👁 Visual learners should draw the cards for the individual letters on another sheet of paper using colored markers (use the Bingo cards for models).

👂 Auditory learners can look at traditional alphabet flash cards, then say the name of the letter. Be sure that you limit the activity to eight to ten at a time. It builds your child's confidence to let her succeed with small groups of letters and then introduce new letters one or two at a time after that.

Mastery occurs when: your child can match the letters when shown an example and begins to name a few letters.

You may want to help your child a little more if: she has problems visually matching the letters. You can try teaching her to trace the letters with her finger. Put the single letters that you use next to the letters on her Bingo card and point out their similarities. Play games that need matching pictures, such as Old Maid, Go Fish, or Memory.

Early Literacy

Young children need to hear stories that reflect what they themselves have felt. Reading should be enjoying, imagining, wondering, and reacting with feeling. Stories for young children should be of all kinds—folktales, funny tales, exciting tales, tales of the wondrous, and stories that tell of everyday things. By reading to children, parents can help them understand that there is a connection between words on a page and the story they hear. Some children will listen for up to ten minutes or more to a favorite book. Some will even insist on having you read a stack of books! Others may be too active to sit still for long.

Let loose when you read to your child; be dramatic with your expressions and your voice. Use a puppet or other prop to help hold your child's attention, or take your child to story time at the public library. When reading to your child, be sure to allow her to choose the stories part of the time; maybe you can take turns choosing the books. Your child will probably have her own favorite books that she will want to hear over and over again.

When your child sits on your lap and follows your finger across the print while you point to the words you say, he learns about written language as well. He learns that the words in a particular written story are always in the same order and on the same page. He will also learn that print goes from left to right and that there are spaces between words. These skills are important when a child begins formal schooling.

Early Literacy Skills	Having Problems?	Quick Tips
Has book-handling skills	Is too rough with books and tears them	Model how you value books and take care of them. Get cardboard books to leave in the play area.
Demonstrates directionality	Starts in the middle or back of books when looking at them	Model left-to-right progression when you read to your child and start from the first page. Try pointing to the page that you are reading. This child just needs more experience with books and story time.
Loves story time	Is not interested in books	Don't force it, but keep trying. Vary your voice or use a puppet to help keep your child's attention. Tell stories, sing songs, and recite rhymes and poems.
Finds ways to relate own experiences to those in the story	Is unable to relate stories to real-life experiences	Connect the story line to your child's real-life experiences. Ask, "Did you ever try this?" "Has anything like that ever happened to you?"

Early Literacy Skills Activities

1 Touch and Tell

Learning happens when: your child tries to identify letters by touch. Put the letters into the gift bag. Blindfold your child. Explain that he should reach into the gift bag, pick up and feel a letter, and try to identify it. After each guess, remove the blindfold so that he can look at the letter and check his answer.

Variations: This variation should be used with children who are just beginning to recognize the letters. Use an alphabet chart to review the letters before your child does the main activity. Ask your child to lay each letter on the table the way it should be written; if this is hard, let him match it to the letter on the alphabet chart.

👋 Have your kinesthetic learner work an alphabet puzzle (the type that has the letters cut out)

👁 Ask your visual learner to extend the alphabet chart by adding the letters drawn from the bag. Provide markers and paper for those who want to attempt to write the alphabet.

👂 Sing a song about the alphabet with your auditory learner, such as "Alligators All Around," by Carole King, or the traditional alphabet song. Ask him to name each letter as you hold it up before putting it away.

Mastery occurs when: your child can identify at least ten of the letters of the alphabet.

You may want to help your child a little more if: he doesn't recognize the letters of the alphabet. Begin by using only the letters in

| TIME: 10 minutes |

MATERIALS
- plastic magnetic letters, or make your own with cardboard
- large gift bag
- blindfold

his own name. This gives extra importance to these letters. Write the first letter of your child's name large enough to cover the paper. Give him some clay and help him work it to soften it so that he can roll it into long snakelike rolls. Use another sheet of paper for rolling the soft clay into long, narrow, snakelike rolls. Have your child use the rolls to cover the lines of the letter that you drew on the other paper, making the letter from clay.

2 Sequencing

TIME: 10 minutes

MATERIALS
■ storybook (for example, *The Mitten*, by Jan Brett)

Learning happens when: your child can retell the story in sequence using the illustrations in the book as a guide. Preview the book with your child by pointing to the title, looking at the pictures on each page, and discussing them. Read the story. Discuss the order of events in the story. Go back through the book and retell the story using the pictures. Your child may want to help tell the story.

Variations: Talk about events in your child's day that occur in a particular order.

✋ Your kinesthetic learner should retell the story using props from around the house. In the case of Jan Brett's *The Mitten,* your child could use one of Dad's or Mom's gloves and toy animals from the story.

👁 Ask your visual learner to hold the book and retell the story by looking at the pictures. After completing the activity, have your child draw or paint her favorite part of the story.

👂 Teach your auditory learner a finger play that involves one of the animals from the story (for example, "Five Green and Speckled Frogs"). Talk about how finger plays go in a particular order also, and recall the sequence.

Mastery occurs when: your child describes the order of events that happen in the story.

You may want to help your child a little more if: she has problems telling the sequence. Play a word game and call it "Tell Me What You Did Today." Ask your child leading questions, such as, "Did you get out of bed or brush your teeth first?" "Did you put on your shoes or socks first?" Use commonsense questions. Continue this type of questioning until your child grows tired of the activity.

3 | Comprehension

Learning happens when: you read the book to your child and then ask questions about the story. You should include questions about setting, characters, and plot. For example:

- *Setting.* "Where do you think this story takes place?" "Do you think this story is about daytime or nighttime?"
- *Characters.* Introduce the characters by taking a picture walk through the book and talking about the illustrations. Ask, "Who do you think is saying good night?"
- *Plot.* "What do you think this story is about?" "How do you know it's time to go to sleep?" "Do all people sleep at night?"

After reading, ask follow-up questions, such as:

"How does the bunny know it's time to go to sleep?"

"How is night different from day?"

"What do you see in the night sky?"

"Do bunnies really sleep in beds?"

Variations: Reread *Goodnight Moon,* pausing before the rhyming words, then asking your child to supply the word that you leave out. Remind him that the words rhyme.

TIME: 10 minutes

MATERIALS
- picture book (for example, *Goodnight Moon,* by Margaret Wise Brown)

✋ Ask your kinesthetic learner to use a stuffed animal to tell you the basic plot of the story. Ask him to relate any personal experiences that may remind him of the book.

👁 After reading the story, ask your visual learner to answer questions by finding the page that shows pictures where specific things happened.

👂 For an auditory learner, choose books with predictable or repetitive text so that he can "read" along with you. After completing the activity, reread the book and ask your child to help you on the parts that he recalls.

Mastery occurs when: your child can answer your questions correctly.

You may want to help your child a little more if: he can't answer your questions about the book. Ask a question about each page immediately after reading it. Repeat this activity using a different book.

4 | Letter Books

TIME: 10 minutes

MATERIALS
▪ two sheets of construction paper
▪ stapler and staples
▪ glue stick
▪ safety scissors
▪ magazines and catalogues

Fold two sheets of paper into fourths and cut both sheets along one of the fold lines. Staple the pages together at the other fold line.

Learning happens when: you make a letter book with your child. Pick a letter with your child and write it on the front of the book. Look through magazines and catalogues with your child to find pictures that begin with this letter. Allow your child to cut out the pictures and glue them onto the pages of the book. If the cutting is hard for your child, you can cut and ask her to glue the pictures. Use a glue stick so that the pages have less chance of sticking together as they dry.

Variations: Have your child make a letter book by putting a letter on each page using a variety of techniques and media—for example, using a letter stamp and stamp pad, using letter stickers, tracing the letter, cutting letters from magazines and gluing them to the page, and tracing the letter in glue and sprinkling glitter on it.

🖐 Write the letter on a sheet of paper and ask your kinesthetic learner to place stickers along the lines until she has a "sticker letter." Complete the activity as directed.

👁 Ask your visual learner to draw, on the last page of the book, a picture of her favorite word that begins with the letter chosen for the activity. After completing the activity, go through the book and write the words for the pictures on each page as your child watches.

👂 Sing the alphabet song with your auditory learner before beginning the activity. Have her practice saying the sound of the letter you have chosen for the activity. Complete the activity and then ask her to "read" the book to you.

Mastery occurs when: your child can name the letter and its sound and can find objects that begin with the letter.

You may want to help your child a little more if: she has problems discriminating the beginning sounds of words. When your child finds a picture in the magazine, emphasize the first sound of the word when you say it. Continue to talk about the sound whenever an opportunity presents itself.

5 | Have You Ever?

TIME: 10 minutes

MATERIALS
- book about feelings (for example, *There's a Nightmare in My Closet,* by Mercer Mayer)
- paper
- crayons or markers

Learning happens when: you read a book to your child about feelings. Sit so that he can see the words and pictures as you read. Read a page of the story, then stop and ask a question: "Did you ever have that feeling?" Listen as your child talks about a similar experience or feeling and relate your own experiences to your child. Ask him to draw a picture about a time when he felt afraid.

Variations: Read any book with a theme that your child can relate to (for example, *Swimmy,* by Leo Lionni; *When Sophie Gets Angry—Really, Really Angry,* by Molly Bang; *The Three Grumpies,* by Tamra Wight).

✋ Ask your kinesthetic learner to show you how he felt under circumstances similar to those in the book. Play a game of facial charades. Name an emotion and ask your child to show it with a facial expression.

👁 Give your visual learner art supplies and encourage him to draw pictures of a time when he was feeling a strong emotion.

👂 Sit with your auditory learner and look at pictures of people in a magazine. Point out their expressions and ask your child about how these people are feeling. Because these learners express themselves well verbally, they often overlook expressions.

Mastery occurs when: your child can relate his own experiences to those of the characters from the book.

You may want to help your child more if: he has problems relating to facial expressions that show emotions. Choose a variety of books that deal with feelings to share with your child. Spend time talking about experiences that make you feel strong emotions.

6 Guess the Rhyme

Learning happens when: your child listens to rhyming words. Talk with your child about rhyming words before you read. Read a rhyme to her. Now reread it leaving out the last word of the rhyme. Let your child fill in the word that goes in the rhyme.

Say two words that rhyme, such as "ran" and "can." Then say, "Now I'm going to say other words that rhyme with ran and can. Here's another one: fan. Now you tell me another word that rhymes with ran, can, and fan." Continue to make rhyming word families as long as it holds your child's interest.

Variations: Use singing rhymes to do the activity (for example, "This Old Man," "Hush Little Baby," "Pop Goes the Weasel," or "Down by the Bay").

Have your kinesthetic learner act out a verse, a stanza, or the entire rhyme. Ask your child to make a face that fits what the character in the rhyme is feeling. Remember that facial expressions bring emotion into the performer's voice.

Ask your visual learner to look through old magazines with you to find pictures that rhyme, such as "jam" and "ham." Your child should cut them out and glue them side by side on a sheet of paper.

This activity is already great as it is for an auditory learner, so use it as an opportunity to help your child learn a new nursery rhyme.

Mastery occurs when: your child hears the ending sounds that rhyme and can distinguish rhyming words from nonrhyming words.

TIME: 10 minutes

MATERIALS
▪ book of nursery rhymes (for example, *My Very First Mother Goose*, by Iona Opie, or *Hey Diddle Diddle! and Other Rhymes*, by Anne E. G. Nydam)

You may want to help your child more if: she doesn't identify rhyming words. You can try using different onsets with the same rhyme. *Onset* is a fancy way of meaning the beginning sound in a word; *rhyme* is the rest of the word. For example, you can start with the word "hat," "h" being the onset and "at" the rhyme. Help your child change only the onset; have her say the new word and "hat" together and point out that they rhyme. You can use "pat," "bat," "rat," "sat," "mat," and "cat." Continue using other words and come back to this activity until your child can identify rhyming words.

7 Read with Me

TIME: 10 minutes

MATERIALS
- book that has predictable print (for example, *Brown Bear, Brown Bear, What Do You See?* by Bill Martin Jr.; *How Many Pets?* by Charlotte Montgomery; *We're Going on a Bear Hunt,* by Michael Rosen)

Learning happens when: you read a book that features predictable print, and your child begins to repeat the words with you as you read. This is an important pre-reading skill. It shows that the child is making connections between printed words and speech, and it builds self-confidence as your child starts to think, "I can read." Predictable print stories are written to contain repetitive phrases or verses, cumulative story lines, or language with rhythm or rhyme. They are a nonthreatening way for your child to build pre-reading skills: if he doesn't know the word, you'll say it.

Variations: Repeat the activity with a variety of books with repetition. Some good examples are *The Big Fat Worm,* by Judy Van Lan; *Who's That Knocking on Christmas Eve?* by Jan Brett; and *The Carrot Seed,* by Ruth Krauss.

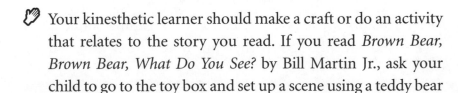 Your kinesthetic learner should make a craft or do an activity that relates to the story you read. If you read *Brown Bear, Brown Bear, What Do You See?* by Bill Martin Jr., ask your child to go to the toy box and set up a scene using a teddy bear

and some other toy animal, then recite what the pages would say if the scene were in the book. He may want to repeat the activity using several different animals.

👁 Ask your visual learner to draw a specific part of the book, such as the animal that he liked best, or to draw an animal that could be added to the book.

👂 Your auditory learner could take turns with you as you read the book to him. You read the page without the repetition and ask your child to "read" the page with the repetition. He may memorize the book and want to "read" it to you. Be sure to praise your child's efforts.

Mastery occurs when: your child enjoys the books, begins to gain confidence in his knowledge about books (such as turning pages, finding the title, and following print as you read), and attempts to read the pages after hearing them read and by looking at the pictures for context clues. Some children may begin to recognize a few sight words.

You may want to help your child more if: he doesn't enjoy the book that you chose. Let him choose the next book (from a group that you preselect). Continue to expose him to books that contain repetition until you find one that he particularly likes. Use inflections of your voice and facial expressions to make the reading more fun. Pick out one word for your child to say during the reading, and change the word during the rereading.

Environmental Learning

Readers raise readers. Books should be available to your child at all times in your home. Go to the library often. Let your child see you reading for enjoyment and for information. Talk about reading. Say

"Let's read to find out," "Let's look up the word to find out what it means," and other similar comments. Your child will learn that books are a resource for finding out new information.

You know from your experience of the toddler years that your child watches everything you do. When your child sees you reading, she not only realizes that it is something that Mommy and Daddy do but also learns essential book-handling skills. She will learn how to distinguish the front of a book from the back, where the title is located, how to turn pages from the right to the left, how to find context clues when looking at illustrations, and countless other things that you do when you read.

End of Preschool Reading Readiness Checklist

Students who are working at the standard level at the end of preschool:

____ Have a large vocabulary

____ Use good grammar often

____ Talk about action in conversation

____ Enjoy rhyming and nonsense words

____ Use regular past tenses of verbs

____ Use "a," "an," and "the" when speaking

____ Ask direct questions

____ Want explanations

____ Recognize their own name in print

Preschool Writing Readiness

6

Because the skills for reading and writing reinforce each other, your child's reading and writing skills will be strengthened if you help your child connect the two skills. Think about the first letter your child gave you. Just a lot of scribbles, right? But you knew exactly what it meant, and more than likely you still have it tucked away in a special place. Your child was beginning to learn to write and knew that those marks on the paper had meaning. Children at this age are making connections between the spoken word and the written word. Once it was believed that children learned to read first and then learned to write. It is now a more common belief that reading and writing develop at the same time and in a related fashion in young children. So your child needs access not only to books but also to paper, pencils, stamps, stamp pads, crayons, and markers. Research shows that children work longer at these activities when their

---

Beginning of Preschool Writing Readiness Checklist

Students who are working at the standard level at the beginning of preschool:

_____ Can tell you their full name

_____ Communicate their needs and wants

_____ Talk to and play with other children

_____ Show interest in stories and books

_____ Participate in songs, finger plays, and chants

_____ Are beginning to reply in full sentences

_____ Put together simple puzzles of four to twelve pieces

_____ Try to cut paper with scissors

_____ Can hold a pencil

_____ Try to write their own name

_____ Can draw a circle

_____ Can draw a face

_____ Draw with their arm and not with the use of small hand movements

activity is open ended rather than a worksheet that has been provided by the teacher. Open-ended activities allow your child to use, demonstrate, and build on knowledge that he or she already has about the subject.

Getting to writing readiness should be fun for four-year-olds. Activities involving the use of small muscles and eye-hand coordination will prepare your child to write. Simple things like sorting buttons; playing with clay, blocks, sidewalk chalk or puzzles; painting using large brushes or fingers; and cutting with safety scissors all help develop these skills.

Four-year-olds generally use large movements. This holds true in their paintings and drawings. This is the time to use sidewalk chalk, large crayons and pencils, markers, and big paintbrushes. Don't be surprised if your child paints the entire paper one color. This is very common and is part of the learning process in painting.

Verbal Communication

Your child has been learning to express his needs and get your attention since he first entered your life. Cry and get fed. Cry again and get held and rocked. This language is also learned by interacting with others. Children gain their communication skills through the speech they hear from their parents as well as from their brothers and sisters, and the more they hear, the more they learn. So be sure to discuss things at the dinner table. Ask your child questions and let him ask questions also. More than likely, the question you will hear most is "Why?" Don't get too frustrated; just do your best to answer his question and be ready to hear "Why?" again. Parents can use language play such as songs, rhymes, and word play to increase their child's communication skills. Children with a larger vocabulary can better access the meaning of words when they are encountered, are more able to comprehend texts read to them, and are more likely to have better language skills in general.

Some adults complain that four-year-olds are wild and difficult to control. They can be, but these behaviors are a part of the child's developmental stage. Most four-year-olds are experiencing strong emotions that are exhibited in their behavior, along with a need for large muscle movements. They can be very dramatic. Young children get frustrated when they can't express their feelings and needs well. Much of this problem is solved when language skills improve. Be sure you practice expressing yourself in front of your child and help your child understand what to say in difficult situations.

Verbal Communication Skills	Having Problems?	Quick Tips
Communicates needs to adults and children	Is shy about asking for help from the teacher or other adults at school	Practice using pretend problems with your child at home. For example, ask, "If your shoe is untied and falls off when you run, how could you get help? Could you ask one of your teachers?"
Understands directions	Is unable to follow directions	Practice two-step directions at home. Ask your child to tell you what she will do first, then second. These should be real directions to complete a task. Move on to three-step directions, and so forth.
Uses a variety of vocabulary when speaking	Doesn't know the meaning of many words	Play word games, sing songs, read books, and talk to your child about words. Daily exposure to new words is the best means for your child to build his vocabulary.
Speaks clearly	Speaks in baby talk	Model correct language when you speak to your child. If you are concerned that she continues to speak in baby talk even after attending preschool, you can check on whether your child has a problem with language development by discussing it with her teacher.

Suppose, for instance, that your child is playing with a toy that another child wants. The other child grabs the toy and walks away. This would of course be upsetting to your child, and many children would grab back or hit the other child. When you observe this type of behavior, it is important to talk through the experience. "What happened here?" "How did you feel when that happened?" "What could you have said?" "What happens when you hit others?" "How do you feel when you get hit?" "How do you think the other child feels?" "Instead of grabbing the toy, you could have said, 'I would like to play with that. Can I have it next?'" "Instead of hitting, what should you have said? You could have said, 'Stop, I get angry when you take my toy.'" Emphasize solving the problem using words. Model that behavior every chance you get and then talk with your child about it.

Verbal Communication Activities

1 Following Directions

TIME: 15 minutes

MATERIALS
- black construction paper
- white crayon
- safety scissors
- glue
- pencil

Before beginning, fold the paper in half. Use the white crayon to draw eight lines (for spider legs) on one half and a circle (for the body) on the other.

Learning happens when: your child follows directions to make a paper spider. Ask your child to cut the circle for the spider's body and the lines for legs. Next ask him to take each leg and curl it around a pencil on one end. This part may be too hard for some children, so help your child if he is having too much difficulty. Then ask your child to use the white crayon to draw two eyes on the circle. Finally, ask your child to turn the spider over and glue on the eight legs, four on each side of its body.

Variations: Use a paper plate for the body instead and color it with a marker. Use construction paper to cut eight straight strips to use for legs. Place a drop of glue on one end of each strip and place it on the paper plate. Hold it for ten seconds to ensure the glue holds.

Kinesthetic learners will love assembling the spider. Ask your child to sing "The Itsy Bitsy Spider" and use his spider to dance to the words of the song.

Visual learners can follow visual directions for this activity if you draw them in sequence. Take a smaller sheet of paper and draw the directions. For example, (1) draw the circle your child is to cut; (2) draw the eight rectangles; (3) show the legs glued to the circle; (4) draw the eyes and mouth.

Ask your auditory learner to repeat the directions before beginning the project and let him listen to songs or poems about spiders while he works. One poem is "Little Miss Muffet." You can find more links to spider songs and poems at www.knowledgeessentials.com.

Mastery occurs when: your child can follow the directions to complete the spider, without becoming frustrated.

You may want to help your child a little more if: he still has problems cutting. Depending on your child's ability, try cutting out five legs yourself and ask your child to cut out three, or any other combination. Check to be sure the scissors he is using are sharp enough and that they fit his hand. *Be sure to use children's safety scissors.* If your child has problems following directions, break the directions up as you give them. Tell him to cut the circle out; after he completes this task, tell him to cut the legs. After he finishes, ask "What did you do first?" (and second). Then give the directions for gluing the legs onto the spider. Ask your child to again restate the steps he has completed. Continue in this way until the project is completed. As this skill begins to develop, try giving two directions; ask your child to repeat them and then follow them before you give other directions.

2 | Going to the Doctor Dramatic Play

TIME: 30 minutes

MATERIALS
- picture book about a visit to the doctor (for example, *The Berenstain Bears Go to the Doctor,* by Stan and Jan Berenstain)
- child's doctor kit

Learning happens when: you show the book to your child, look at the pictures together, and discuss them. Read the story and then look back at the pictures to discuss the tools the doctor uses in the story. Let your child play with the doctor kit for a while, and reread the story later.

Variations: Ask your child to retell the story by looking at the pictures. Talk about what she should do when you are away from home and she feels sick. Help your child set up a "hospital" using her toys and let her play "doctor."

- Your kinesthetic learner will use the different "tools" as she pretends to be a doctor to "sick" toys.

- Visual learners will like to use the illustrations in the book to retell the story or show different ways doctors help us.

- An auditory learner can tell you all about a time when she was sick and how a doctor helped her.

Mastery occurs when: your child can identify some tools doctors use and uses their correct names during play with a doctor kit, and when she can explain some of the ways doctors help children and adults.

You may want to help your child a little more if: she is very afraid to go to the doctor. It could be helpful to allow lots of playtime with the doctor's kit. Ask your child questions about this playtime in order to help her develop a better understanding of what doctors do for people. You could try taking turns being the patient and the doctor while playing with the doctor's kit. Role-playing difficult situations can help a young child deal with them better. Ask your child what happened to the Berenstain Bears when they went to the doctor. Did they overcome their fear? How?

3 | Big Red Barn

Learning happens when: you show the book to your child and look through it to discuss the illustrations. Read the book. Look back at the illustrations and discuss the various animals. Sing a song about farm animals (for example, "Old MacDonald Had a Farm"). Ask your child to sort the animals and then explain his sorting rule to you (big and little, furry and not furry, scary and not scary, and so on).

Variations: Give the book to your child; let him match a model animal with each animal in the book and name them all.

- Your kinesthetic learner can use the model animals to retell the story.

- Your visual learner should hold the book and name the farm animals in the illustrations. You can ask him to draw a picture of a farm or favorite farm animals, or find farm animals in coloring books.

- Your auditory learner will enjoy singing the song and renaming the farm animals.

Mastery occurs when: your child can name farm animals and use vocabulary from the book in conversation.

TIME: 20 minutes

MATERIALS
- picture book about life on a farm (for example, *Big Red Barn,* by Margaret Wise Brown)
- package of plastic farm animals

You may want to help your child a little more if: he finds the tasks too tedious. Reread the book periodically and discuss it with your child. Ask, for example, "What do you remember about the chicken?" or "Can you name all the animals on the cover of the book?" Or make up riddles about farm animals and see if your child can answer them. For example, "I have fur, four legs, and say moo. What am I?"

4   Naming Foods

TIME: 10 minutes

MATERIALS
▪ flannel board foods, toy foods, or real foods
▪ bag for the vegetables

Learning happens when: you sing the vegetable song shown here (sung to the tune of "Down by the Station") and talk about gardens in general and any gardens that she might be familiar with in particular.

Down by the garden, early in the morning, see the red tomatoes all in a row. See Farmer Brown going out to pick some, pick, pick, pick—off we go.

Down by the garden, early in the morning, see the yellow corn all in a row. See Farmer Brown going out to pick some, pick, pick, pick—off we go.

Down by the garden, early in the morning, see the purple eggplants all in a row. See Farmer Brown going out to pick some, pick, pick, pick—off we go.

Down by the garden, early in the morning, see the green beans all in a row. See Farmer Brown going out to pick some, pick, pick, pick—off we go.

Down by the garden, early in the morning, see the orange carrots all in a row. See Farmer Brown going out to pick some, pick, pick, pick—off we go.

Down by the garden, early in the morning, see the brown potatoes all in a row. See Farmer Brown going out to pick some, pick, pick, pick—off we go.

Say to your child, "Today we'll play a listening game. I'll sing a song. You listen carefully, then pick up the vegetables that I'm singing about and put them into the bag." You can vary the song according to the foods that you have, and if you do this activity again, mix up the order.

Variations: Do the same activity, but use flower gardens instead of food. Try to locate flowers in your neighborhood or a nearby park (for example, "Down by the garden, early in the morning, see the white daisies all in a row. See Mrs. Brown going out to smell some, sniff, sniff, sniff—off we go.")

✋ Your kinesthetic learner should count the foods that are in the bag as she takes them out of the bag and arranges the objects in the "garden" to play the game again.

👁 Ask your visual learner to look into the bag, remove the vegetable that she put in first, and continue to remove the remaining vegetables in sequential order.

👂 Your auditory learner can sing the song while you follow the directions. As you take the vegetable from the garden, your child should describe the way it looks. You may need to provide some adjectives for this task.

Mastery occurs when: your child listens to the song and is able to connect the items in the song to the items she puts in the bag.

You may want to help your child a little more if: she doesn't know which vegetable to pick up. You should explain the directions again and point out that the color words describe the vegetable. Emphasize the importance of listening to the song and do the activity again.

5 | Describe the Toy

TIME: 15 minutes

MATERIALS
■ 5–10 toys that belong to your child

Learning happens when: you explain that words can describe objects. Hold up a toy and describe it using its name, texture, color, and use. Put the toy down. Next say, "This time, listen carefully to what I say, then show me the toy I described."

Variations: Take turns with your child describing the objects.

- Your kinesthetic learner should hold the objects as he describes them to you.
- Play I Spy with your visual learner.
- Ask your auditory learner to repeat the words used to describe the object.

Mastery occurs when: your child starts to use more than one word to describe objects.

You may want to help your child a little more if: he has problems describing the objects in the activity. Ask questions that will guide him to thinking about more of the attributes of that object in order to give better descriptions.

6 | Hokey Pokey

TIME: 10 minutes

Learning happens when: you sing "The Hokey Pokey" to your child and demonstrate how to play the game.

Variation: Sing the song "Head, Shoulders, Knees, and Toes" and use both hands to touch the body parts as you sing. Start at a slow tempo and sing a little faster each time you start again. Mix up the body parts to keep it interesting.

Head and shoulders, knees and toes, knees and toes,

Head and shoulders, knees and toes, knees and toes,

And eyes and ears and mouth and nose,

Head and shoulders, knees and toes, knees and toes.

✋ Have your kinesthetic learner make up a new motion for the song and demonstrate it to you.

👁 For your visual learner, make signs with pictures of the various body parts in the song and hold them up to tell your child which body part to put in next.

👂 Have your auditory learner use the variation activity.

Mastery occurs when: your child can sing along and perform the correct motions.

You may want to help your child a little more if: she can't sing along and perform the motions. Try teaching one or two verses only and then adding others as your child succeeds.

7 Rhyming Words

Learning happens when: you read the story to your child and ask him to listen for words that sound alike (rhyme). Read a couple of pages at a time and then have him identify two words that sound alike. Ask your child what letters or sounds the rhyming words have in common.

TIME: 20 minutes

MATERIALS
▪ *Giraffes Can't Dance,* by Giles Andreae

Variations: Teach your child a rhyming song. You can use a favorite from your childhood or use "This Old Man."

This old man, he played one,

He played knick-knack on my thumb.

With a knick-knack, paddy whack, give a dog a bone,
This old man came rolling home.
This old man, he played two,
He played knick-knack on my shoe.
This old man, he played three,
He played knick-knack on my knee.
This old man, he played four,
He played knick-knack on my door.
This old man, he played five,
He played knick-knack on my hive.
This old man, he played six,
He played knick-knack on my sticks.
This old man, he played seven,
He played knick-knack up in heaven.
This old man, he played eight,
He played knick-knack on my gate.
This old man, he played nine,
He played knick-knack on my spine.
This old man, he played ten,
He played knick-knack once again.
With a knick-knack, paddy whack, give a dog a bone,
This old man came rolling home.

Sing one verse at a time and ask your child to listen for rhyming words. Stop to identify the rhyming words in the stanza. Your child should be able to identify the next rhyming words.

- Have your kinesthetic learner act out the verse as you read it aloud; then have him identify the two words that rhyme.

- If possible, have your visual learner point to the pictures of the words that rhyme.

👂 Auditory learners will enjoy the main activity as described. Use the variation activity.

Mastery occurs when: your child can identify the rhyming sounds.

You may want to help your child a little more if: he can't identify the rhyming sounds. Try emphasizing the rhyming words as you read them.

8 Call Me

Learning happens when: your child pretends to call a relative, such as her grandma. Ask your child to tell "Grandma" about what she did that day or what she ate for dinner.

Variations: Talk about the meaning of the word *emergency*. Describe some examples of emergencies and talk about calling 911 for help. Show your child the numbers 911 and practice calling for help on a toy phone or one that is disconnected. Describe different scenarios and ask your child to tell you whether each one is an emergency or not.

🖐 Make sure your kinesthetic learner gets to push the buttons on the phone to call Grandma.

👁 Give your visual learner a picture of the person she is calling. She might find it easier to talk if she can actually see the person.

👂 Let your auditory learner make a real phone call.

Mastery occurs when: your child can talk to someone and tell him or her about the day or an activity.

You may want to help your child a little more if: she doesn't talk on the phone. Prompt her about what to say.

TIME: 10 minutes

MATERIALS
- play phone

9 Singing Directions

TIME: 10 minutes

Learning happens when: you teach the song "If You're Happy and You Know It" to your child. This song will allow your child to follow directions in a fun way.

Variations: Teach your child to play the game Mother, May I? Your child will have to remember to say "Mother, may I?" and then move as described in the command. You may want to reward good listening with a snack after you finish playing.

🖐 Let your kinesthetic learner add more actions and directions to follow.

👁 Demonstrate the actions to your visual learner before you sing each verse.

👂 Auditory learners will enjoy the main activity as described and the variation activity.

Mastery occurs when: your child can perform all the actions correctly.

You may want to help your child a little more if: he feels frustrated as he does this activity. Do one verse on one day. Practice the same verse the next day and then ask your child if he would like to do another verse.

10 Twister

TIME: 15 minutes

MATERIALS
■ Twister game

Learning happens when: your child plays Twister with you. This is a fun way for your child to learn to follow and give directions.

Variations: Show your child how to build a tower using four alphabet blocks, wooden cubes, or small cardboard boxes. Describe what you are doing, then give the cubes to her and ask her to do the same. If this is hard for her, help out by holding the bottom cube.

- 🖐 Your kinesthetic learner will love doing the activity as described. Also try the variation activity.

- 👁 Have your visual learner watch someone else play the game, then let her take her turn.

- 👂 Auditory learners will enjoy the main activity as described.

Mastery occurs when: your child can follow the directions correctly.

You may want to help your child a little more if: she feels frustrated as she does this activity. Modify the game to involve only the arms or the legs.

Emergent Writing

Create a special place for your child to write. Make sure everything is easy for him to access. Be sure to provide paper, pencils, markers, crayons, coloring books, chalk and chalkboard—the sky's the limit. Children refine their knowledge of the written language by drawing and play-writing. Encourage your child to talk about this play-writing by saying things like "Tell me about that." Experimenting with drawing and writing is an important step in developing both writing readiness and reading readiness. Your child may show you scribbles and ask you to read them. Take this as an opportunity to model writing for your child. She may ask how to make a certain letter; when this happens, be sure to take the time to show her how to do it. Put it where she can see it again in order to practice writing it.

Proficiency in written language requires time, practice, and patience. Writing skills develop and become more sophisticated as children use them for meaningful purposes. You can provide alphabet stamps and stamp pads for your child to use, tactile alphabet puzzles, and an alphabet chart. Cutting and pasting, drawing, painting, and playing with small toys all engage the eye-hand coordination that writing requires.

Emergent Writing Skills	Having Problems?	Quick Tips
Draws pictures to communicate	Doesn't want to draw	Allow your child to practice with finger paints, drawing in shaving cream or sand, playing with sidewalk chalk, and painting at the easel with large brushes and large paper. Providing a variety of writing utensils will encourage your child to explore this skill.
Play-writes	Is not interested in trying to write	Let your child pick out markers or glitter pens as well as special paper to write on. Have your child help write a shopping list. Be sure to let him add a few things to the list. Pour salt in a pan and have him copy your example of a word by "writing" it in the salt.
Attempts to write name	Asks me to write his name	Write the name so that your child can watch you writing—this is good modeling. He will eventually try writing it. Offer opportunities to trace lots of things: shapes, letters, and straight and curved lines. Mazes provide practice in making marks that show the way. Let your child play with stamps and stamp pads.
Understands that there are many reasons to use written language	Draws pictures instead of writing	Write shopping lists with your child, then take her shopping and use the list. Talk about the process with your child. Cook together and use a recipe that you read and do step by step.
Understands that writing provides information	Doesn't pay attention to writing	Write your child's name to identify his belongings.

Emergent Writing Activities

1 | Greeting Cards

TIME: 15 minutes

MATERIALS
- crayons
- markers
- paper
- stickers

Learning happens when: you talk with your child about different types of cards that come in the mail. Show him some examples of cards you have received. Discuss the way the cards look and read the messages to your child. Ask him who might be some people who would enjoy getting a card. Have your child choose someone to make a card for. Fold the paper in half to make the card. Write a sentence frame on another piece of paper. Take turns with your child using it to practice making sentences that could go in the card. For example: "Happy birthday, _____. I hope you have a _____ day. Love, _____." Copy the frame onto the card and let your child dictate words for the blanks.

✋ Have your kinesthetic learner decorate his card using art materials, such as glitter, sequins, colored paper, lace, and pictures from magazines. He should put the card into an envelope and go with you to mail it.

👁 When you show your visual learner some of the cards that he or the family has received, ask him to look carefully at the picture on the card and guess what the occasion was for receiving it.

👂 After your auditory learner completes the card, have him "read" each of the sentences with you.

Mastery occurs when: your child makes a card for someone and tells you why he wants to give the card to that person. After you make a sentence frame that fits the reason for the card, he completes the sentence frame and "reads" it to you.

You may want to help your child a little more if: he has problems finishing the sentence frame. Read a book about fish to your child (such as *Swimmy*, by Leo Lionni). Write a simple sentence frame like: "Fish are _____. Fish live in _____." Ask your child to fill in the blanks by dictating the words while you write them in the frame. Practice this activity several times.

2 Me Art

TIME: 10 minutes

MATERIALS
- finger paint (your child's favorite color)
- cookie sheet
- 12 × 18-inch sheet of construction paper
- marker
- clear contact paper
- paint smock or old clothes
- newspapers

Spread old newspapers over the top of a table or desk, lay the cookie sheet down, and pour out the finger paint.

Learning happens when: your child builds writing readiness skills by working with finger paint. Put old clothes on your child or use a paint smock and allow your child free play with the finger paint. When your child grows tired of playing in the paint, help her make handprints on the construction paper and let them dry. Write your child's name above the handprints using a marker. When the handprints are dry, cover the construction paper on both sides with clear contact paper and let your child use it as her personal place mat.

Variations: Using a letter-shaped cookie cutter—preferably your child's first initial—trace the letter all over the construction paper and let your child fill in the letters with finger paint.

Give your kinesthetic learner a paintbrush and let her paint using her favorite color. Don't be surprised if she paints the entire page. After it dries, write "[Color] is [child's name]'s favorite color." Cover with clear contact paper and use it as a place mat or hang it up as refrigerator art.

👁 For your visual learner, write out your child's name on a separate sheet of paper as a model and ask her to match the letters and to write out her own name with the stamps. If this is too frustrating, let her just use the first letter of her name to decorate the construction paper. Use a marker to write her name on the paper.

👂 For your auditory learner, make up an alliteration sentence using her name (for example, "Sweet Sara sings so softly"). Teach this sentence to your child and exaggerate the beginning sounds.

Mastery occurs when: your child experiments with finger paint as an emergent writing skill and can recognize some of the letters in her own name.

You may want to help your child a little more if: your child cannot recognize any letters in her name. Talk about the letter that comes first. Trace the initial letter with the child's finger. Count the letters.

3 Add-Ons

Learning happens when: your child plays a writing completion game. Using a chalkboard, draw simple shapes or objects with an obvious missing part, such as a square with a missing side or a stick man without arms. Have your child draw on the missing part. Now try this with your child's name. Write out his first name so that he can visualize a correct model. Next, draw part of the first letter of his name and ask him to look at the model and complete the letter. Try this again, but leave out a different part of the same letter. Once your child gets the hang of this, move on to the other letters of his name.

TIME: 10 minutes

MATERIALS
▪ chalkboard and chalk

Variations: Repeat the same activity using crayons, markers, or finger paints, or go outside to the driveway or sidewalk to use the chalk. Read stories to your child about a child learning to write, such as *Leo the Late Bloomer,* by Robert Kraus.

🖐 Write your kinesthetic learner's name on a large sheet of construction paper. Show him how to use a glue stick to trace the letters and place sequins on the letter to create a jeweled name.

👁 For your visual learner, use a page from a photo album as a reusable sheet of paper. Using a dry erase marker, write your child's name across the top as a model. Underneath, draw the beginning parts of each letter of his name and use dots or dashes to complete it. Give him the dry erase marker to connect the dots or dashes in his name. Use a paper towel or cloth to erase. Save this photo album page for repeated use in this and other activities.

👂 Give your auditory learner oral directions on how to draw letters as you demonstrate and give oral directions as he writes the letter. Together say the sound of each letter. Continue until all letters of the name are written. Segment his name by saying the sounds of each letter in his name and blend the sounds together to say the name.

Mastery occurs when: your child begins to recognize some of the letters in his name and correctly writes the shape of some of the letters.

You may want to help your child a little more if: he takes too much time with the activity and loses interest in the project. Stop and finish it later.

4 Magnetic Name

Write your child's name on sticky notes, using one sheet for each letter of your child's name. Arrange the sheets in order on a metal surface, such as a refrigerator or file cabinet. Find the magnetic letters that spell your child's name and put them into the plastic bag.

Learning happens when: your child matches the letters on the sticky notes to magnetic letters to spell out her name. Explain to your child that the letters on the sticky notes spell her name and that she should find the magnetic letters that match those on the sticky notes. As she finds them, place the magnetic letters under the sticky notes.

Variations: As your child improves in "writing" her name with the magnetic letters, remove one written letter and replace it with a blank sheet. This will challenge your child to recall the letter left out. Next, try removing two letters and so on until your child can recall the order of all the letters. Be patient with this activity. It should take place over a period of several days or weeks.

🖐 After you complete the main activity, give your kinesthetic learner Wikki sticks and a sheet of paper with her name written in large letters. Wikki sticks are waxy and slightly sticky colored sticks that you can find in toy stores or stores that sell teaching supplies. Ask your child to follow the model and bend the Wikki sticks into the shapes of the letters to spell her name.

👁 Before you begin the main activity, give your visual learner the bag of letters and ask her to find the letters that are in her name. If this is too difficult for your child, help her by referring her to a model of her name spelled out.

TIME: 10 minutes

MATERIALS
- 2 packages of magnetic letters (depending on your child's name)
- sticky notes
- small plastic bag

For your auditory learner, write three words, one of which is your child's name, on a large sheet of paper. Use words that begin with different letters. Do this four or five times before you begin the activity. Sing an alphabet song, then ask your child to locate his name in the first group of words and point to it. You can circle it. Repeat this with each of the other groups of words.

Mastery occurs when: your child begins to recognize her own name in print.

You may want to help your child a little more if: she has a long name that makes the activity too difficult. This is not an easy activity; you may need to repeat it many times, so show patience with your child.

5 Lists

TIME: 15 minutes

MATERIALS
■ newspaper grocery ads (and coupons if you use them)
■ marker
■ paper
■ pencil

Learning happens when: you use your weekly shopping trip as an opportunity to help your child develop reading and writing skills. Talk with him about the things you need to buy. Ask him to look through the ads to find the things that are on sale this week. He can "read" the pictures and some brand names to make suggestions for your trip. Talk as you write your list so that your child can watch you and make the connection between the spoken and written words. Ask your child to look through your coupons to select the ones you can use. While shopping, let your child see you read the list and ask him to help you gather the items on the list.

Variations: Use this activity to plan a birthday party, holiday meal, or family outing.

👋 Complete the main activity and ask your kinesthetic learner to sort the shapes of the groceries that you bought before helping put them away.

👁 When you are in a grocery store, ask your visual learner to get specific products. This gives your child extra practice in "reading" the labels and logos.

👂 Ask your auditory learner to tell you about three things that he would like you to get while you're at the store. Ask him to explain his reasons. If the reasons are acceptable, let the child locate the items and buy them for him. While you're shopping, be sure to ask such questions as, "Now what do we need on this aisle? Did I get everything we needed?" Read back over the list while the two of you check the cart for the items.

Mastery occurs when: your child understands some reasons that people make lists.

You may want to help your child more if: he has problems "reading" labels on food products. Talk about the labels as you put the groceries away. Point out the colors and specific pictures on each label. Point to the name as you read it to your child.

6 Sticker Writing

Learning happens when: your child "writes" her name using stickers. Give your child a sheet of paper and the sticker pages. Write your child's name on the paper and then have your child place the corresponding letter stickers on the paper. Continue the activity with a few other words that are meaningful to her.

TIME: 15 minutes

MATERIALS
- alphabet stickers
- paper

Variations: Write your child's name on a large sheet of construction paper. Help her trace the letters with glue and lay the paper on a cookie sheet. She should sprinkle glitter over the glue and gently shake the paper to distribute the glitter. Let it dry laying flat, then attach it to the wall or door of her room at her eye level.

✋ Kinesthetic learners will enjoy the main activity as described.

👁 Visual learners will enjoy making their names by gluing small items that start with the same sound as their name into the letters (for example, sand for Sid, jelly beans for Joe, or mini marshmallows for Mary).

👂 Read her name or a word aloud to your auditory learner and have her repeat it and say the name of each letter as she places it on the paper.

Mastery occurs when: your child can place the sticker letters in the correct order to spell her name or another word.

You may want to help your child more if: she can't place the stickers in the correct order. Try writing one letter at a time and then having your child find that letter before going to the next one.

7 Write On, Wipe Off

TIME: 10 minutes

MATERIALS
- dry erase marker board
- dry erase markers

Learning happens when: you tell your child a word and then write the word on the dry erase board. Tell your child that this is how we write words. Have your child use another color of dry erase marker to trace the word.

Variations: You could also make dots for your child to connect to form each letter.

✋ Kinesthetic learners will enjoy the main activity as described.

👁 In addition to the original activity, show your visual learner a picture of the object that you are writing the word for.

👂 Read the word aloud to your auditory learner and have him repeat the word. Say the names of the letters as your child is tracing them.

Mastery occurs when: your child can trace the letters for the word.

You may want to help your child more if: he can't trace the letters correctly. Try having him write one letter at a time.

8 | Glue your Name

Use the glue to write your child's name on a sheet of paper. Allow time for it to dry.

TIME: 10 minutes

MATERIALS
▪ paper
▪ glue

Learning happens when: your child traces the glue letters with her fingers.

Variations: Peel the letters off the paper and mix them up. Have your child place them in the correct order.

✋ Your kinesthetic learner will enjoy both the main activity and the variation.

👁 Visual learners will enjoy using markers to trace over the letters of their names. Call the activity Rainbow Names and encourage them to use all the marker colors in the box.

👂 As your auditory learner is tracing the letters, say the name of each letter.

Mastery occurs when: your child can trace the letters of her name.

You may want to help your child more if: she can't trace the letters correctly. Try writing one letter at a time.

9 | Which Way Do I Go?

TIME: 10 minutes

MATERIALS
- pencil
- paper

On the handwriting paper, place a star where your child should begin a letter and another star where the letter should end.

Learning happens when: your child writes his name on the handwriting paper. Give him the paper prepared as described. Start with the beginning letter of his first name. Tell him that he is to start the letter at the first star and end it at the second star. Continue the procedure until your child has written his name from left to right.

Variations: Place the stars farther apart and have your child write a whole word between the two stars.

🖐 Kinesthetic learners will enjoy the main activity as described.

👁 Write your visual learner's name on a sheet of paper for her to use as an example for the activity as described.

👂 Give your auditory learner step-by-step directions in placing a letter between the stars in sequential order.

Mastery occurs when: your child can correctly write the letters in his name from left to right.

You may want to help your child more if: he can't write the letters correctly from left to right. Draw an arrow at the top of the paper demonstrating what direction to go next.

Environmental Learning

By this time your child has begun to "read" signs from fast-food restaurants, toy stores, and the grocery store. She will recognize labels or brand names from various products and can probably recognize informational signs, such as signs for restrooms that show pictures of boys or girls. She may begin to notice her own name in print from labels on school supplies and clothing. Encourage your child to "write" often. Tracing, mimicking, scribbling, and coloring familiar shapes, letters, and words refine small motor skills and build confidence. Have a (to-do, grocery, or errand) list? Let your child check things off the list. Point to what should be checked off, say the word, and let your child mark away!

End of Preschool Writing Readiness Checklist

Students who are working at the standard level at the end of preschool:

____ Follow simple rules and instructions

____ Use a variety of strategies to problem-solve in class

____ Initiate activities in the classroom

____ Communicate needs, wants, and thoughts in primary language

____ Pay attention during teacher-directed group activities

____ Begin to make letter-sound associations

____ Engage in conversation (complete sentences, turn-taking)

____ Can recall activities and explain sequences of events

____ Participate in art activities that involve eye-hand coordination

____ Recognize own name in print

____ Persist with self-selected emergent writing activity for fifteen minutes

____ Appropriately express range of emotions

____ Begin to recognize signs in the environment

____ Try to copy words

____ Use letter-like forms, scribbles, or random letters to write messages

Preschool Math 7

For many children, this will be their first year in a classroom. The preschool classroom is one where children will be exploring and learning through play. Although you may think that playing and learning are separate entities, young children learn a great deal through play. It is not appropriate at this age for children to sit for long periods of time doing activities on paper. There will be times when preschoolers are sitting and listening, and there will be times when they are doing tasks on paper, but most of their time will be spent learning through play and exploration.

Beginning of Preschool Math Checklist

Students who are working at the standard level at the beginning of preschool:

___ Compare objects and recognize more and less

___ Count to four or higher

___ Understand size differences (for example, big and small, long and short)

___ Demonstrate one-to-one correspondence with objects

Many underlying concepts in math are built through play. A preschool classroom's math program usually consists of large group activities and exploration at centers or areas in the classroom that provide the opportunity to explore a concept. Large group activities usually occur during "calendar time." At this time preschoolers sing counting songs, learn about the days of the week and months of the year, look at the next number on the number line, and so on. Calendar time provides structure and routine while teaching many concepts. In addition to calendar time, there will probably be a designated time during the day when your child will go to centers for free exploration. Some centers may be permanent, including housekeeping, the sand table, and the block center. Other centers are temporary. These centers usually coincide with a concept or theme that is being taught in the classroom. Temporary centers last from a few days to a few weeks. Center activities include painting, building blocks, listening center (songs, recorded story books), and puzzles. Most of the pre-kindergarten math concepts will be taught through calendar time and centers.

Preschoolers are typically very concrete in their thinking. They have to be able to use their senses to understand a concept. As adults, we can think of the number five, for example, in many different ways. We can think of five concretely (five objects), abstractly (a nickel), and symbolically (a numeral, a word, a math sentence). We can think of many ways to make five, through addition, subtraction, multiplication, division, money, and so on. In contrast, preschoolers mostly think of five concretely as five objects. It is only after they have mastered a concept concretely that young children can move to abstract and symbolic thinking. If your child is having trouble with any concept, he must be able to understand that concept concretely before he can cross the bridge to abstract or symbolic thinking.

Because young children need concrete experiences, early childhood classrooms have manipulatives available. Manipulatives are any objects that children can count or handle. Manipulatives found in the early childhood classroom include dice, cubes, blocks, tangrams, clocks, attribute blocks (small wooden shapes, with like shape painted the same color), spinners, and cards. You have many manipulatives in your home that you can use to help your child with math. Examples include a calendar, a deck of cards, dice, dried beans, and measuring cups. Manipulatives are very important in helping your child experience math concretely, which is why many of the activities in this chapter use manipulatives or have your child actively doing something. This experience will help lay the foundation for the abstract thinking that will come in the later elementary grades.

The preschool math curriculum includes the broad areas of number sense, patterns, geometry, and measurement.

Number Sense and Patterns

Developing number sense is vital for success in mathematics. Number sense is an understanding of the underlying rules and patterns found in mathematics. Number sense includes seeing how numbers relate to one another and how they can be put together and taken apart. Children who develop number sense see math as logical and orderly. They understand how the number system works, and they can quickly determine how a new concept fits into the math scheme. Children who do not develop number sense often have a fragmented view of math. They may be able to follow a procedure or learn a concept by rote, but they won't understand the "why" of math and cannot fit the pieces together. Math will become more difficult for a child without number sense. You can help your child develop number sense through play, games, and activities. Your child may need more time to develop number sense; if that is the case, give him or her extra time at home to work with manipulatives and think concretely. Preschool classrooms develop number sense by engaging children in counting, pairing, sorting, and classifying objects.

Another important skill that will be developed in math is working with patterns. Patterns are really the precursor to algebraic thinking. Our world is filled with patterns, and preschoolers will learn how to identify and extend them. They work with patterns by sorting and classifying objects into groups and by exploring different patterns, such as color and geometric patterns. Exploring patterns will help children beyond the math classroom. Patterns are found in virtually every subject, from math and science to language arts and social studies. Developing your child's ability to recognize patterns will help him or her across all subject areas in school.

Number Sense and Pattern Skills	Having Problems?	Quick Tips
Counts up to ten objects	Has trouble counting objects	Take every opportunity to count with your child. Count the number of steps it takes to get to another room, the number of eggs in the refrigerator, the forks needed for dinner, and so on. If your child is having trouble with rote counting, there are many counting songs that help children learn to count. Look in the children's music section of any major music retailer.
Understands ordinal numbers (first, second, third, etc.)	Has trouble understanding ordinal numbers	When you are asking your child to do something, ask her to do two things. Specify which thing to do first and which to do second. For example, you can say, "I need you to put your pajamas on first and then brush your teeth." Praise your child when she successfully completes the tasks in the order you ask. When your child asks for a snack, ask him to carefully watch what you do to prepare it. For example, make a peanut butter sandwich, then question your child about the order of steps used to make the sandwich. You can ask, "Did I open the bread or spread the peanut butter first? What did I put away last?"
Connects numbers to the numerals that represent them	Does not know which numeral goes with which number	Help your child notice numbers in his environment. Numbers are everywhere. Point out the numbers you see, such as the numbers in an address, on a telephone keypad, or on a sports jersey. If you name the number your child is seeing, eventually your child will connect the name of the number to its numeral.
Understands the meaning of addition and subtraction	Does not understand that adding increases the number of items, whereas subtracting decreases the number of items	Your child does not need to know how to use the operations of addition and subtraction, but she needs to understand the concept of making a set bigger by adding or making a set smaller by subtracting. Look for opportunities to highlight this concept. For example, if your child announces that she is finished eating dinner, but you think she needs to eat a little more, ask your child to take five more bites. After your

Number Sense and Pattern Skills	Having Problems?	Quick Tips
		child takes one bite, ask her how many bites are left. Continue for each bite. If you are putting stamps on several envelopes to be mailed, note with your child how many are stamped and how many are left to be stamped. There are many opportunities in daily life to emphasize the concept of adding and subtracting. Children learn a lot through little teachable moments.
Notices and explains patterns	Has trouble noticing patterns or verbalizing a pattern	It is probably easier to start with color patterns. During snack time you can give your child permission to play with his food to explore patterns. This works best with colored candies, raisins and peanuts, different-shaped crackers, or carrot and celery sticks. Start a simple two-color pattern, such as red-yellow-red-yellow-red-yellow. Ask your child to name the colors in the pattern. Then ask him to tell you what comes next in the pattern. If your child is correct, let him eat the pattern. Once your child is comfortable with this activity, you can go on a pattern search in your house. Look for things that have a color or geometric pattern. You will probably be amazed at all the patterns that your child finds around the house.
Sorts, orders, and classifies objects	Has trouble placing like objects together	Ask your child to help around the house. For example, when unloading the dishwasher, ask your child to sort the silverware into the sorting tray. When folding laundry, ask your child to go through the pile of laundry and put all the shirts together, all the pants together, etc. There are many opportunities for your child to sort objects.

Number Sense and Patterns Activities

1 How Many Coins?

Time: 10 minutes

MATERIALS
- cup full of assorted coins
- die

Learning happens when: your child uses the die and coins to play a counting game. Ask your child to roll the die. He may need to count the dots on the die to determine the number. Then he needs to get that many coins from the cup. Continue until he has removed all the coins from the cup.

Variations: This can be a two-player game. Each will take turns rolling the die and taking that number of coins from the cup. Continue until the coins are used. Once all the coins are out of the cup, each player's coins are counted. The player with more coins wins.

Kinesthetic learners can pick up two different coins, compare and contrast their looks and sizes, then sort them into groups of like coins.

Visual learners can begin to identify the coins in the cup by name. Help them arrange the coins into lines to form a real graph (one line of pennies, one of nickels, one of dimes, and one of quarters) and ask them to tell you about the visual comparison. Which line has the most coins? Which has the fewest? How many nickels are there? Dimes? Quarters?

Auditory learners can describe the coins to you, count the total aloud, and sing a finger play, such as "Five Little Ducks," "Five Little Monkeys Jumping on the Bed," or "One, Two Buckle My Shoe."

Mastery occurs when: your child can successfully count the number of coins determined by the die.

You may want to help your child a little more if: he is having trouble with the die, especially when having to count both the dots and the coins. If your child is having problems, ask him to roll the die, but you call the number of dots. Then he gathers that number of coins. If your child is having trouble counting the coins, start with smaller numbers. Ask him to pull out one, two, or three coins. Once he is successful, move on to the more difficult numbers.

2 | How Many in a Room?

On each of the five index cards, draw a picture of one of the following: a window, door, chair, pillow, and mirror.

TIME: 15 minutes

MATERIALS
- 5 index cards
- markers or crayons

Learning occurs when: your child counts the number of various items or objects in a room. Go into one room in the house. Shuffle the cards and ask your child to draw one card. Next, ask her to count the number of whatever object is shown on the card. Do not worry if the room does not have the object shown on the card. Zero is a perfectly acceptable answer if it is true. Go into a different room and ask your child to draw another card. Count the objects in the room. Continue until all five cards have been used.

Variations: This activity can be extended with questions for your child, such as "Does the dining room have more windows than the living room?" Pose a question and ask your child to find the answer.

With your kinesthetic learner, play a "Mother May I?" type of game involving listening and moving. Ask your child to listen as you say a number (one through ten) and name a movement (for example, clap, snap your fingers, baby steps, hop) that she should do to show the number that you say.

- 👁 Give your visual learner colored markers and papers that have the numerals 1 through 5 written on them and ask her to draw pictures on the papers that show the number written on them.

- 👂 After your auditory learner has completed the activity, say a number to her and ask her to use building blocks or attribute blocks to show you that many items, then count them together to check.

Mastery occurs when: your child can successfully count the number of specific objects in a room.

You may want to help your child a little more if: she is having trouble counting the objects in a room. It may be overwhelming for your child to change objects from room to room. Ask her to draw one card. If the card shows a window, for example, move from room to room counting only windows.

3 | What's First?

TIME: 10 minutes

MATERIALS
- 3 different small objects

Learning happens when: your child arranges the three objects in the order you specify. The objects can be anything. For example, give your child a ball, a toy car, and a pencil. Ask him to put the objects in a specific order, using the words "first," "second," and "third." You could say, for example, "Please put the car first, the ball second, and the pencil third." Praise your child for correctly arranging the objects. Try this again, but ask him to arrange the objects in a different order. When this becomes dull, let your child be the one to specify the order of objects so that you can arrange them. Finally, put the objects in any order and ask your child to name the object that is in a specific position. For example, you would ask, "Which object is second?"

Variations: Once your child is comfortable completing this activity with three items, gather five objects and try the activity again. Then ask your child to name the object in a specific position. Trade roles and let your child test you. Throw in a couple of wrong answers to see if your child catches your mistakes.

✋ Let your kinesthetic learner pick out toys that he wants to use and bring them to you. Ask him to put them in a line, then question him about the positions of the toys and let him indicate the answer by touching the toy.

👁 When you are in line at a store with your visual learner, ask him to name your position in the line.

👂 Line up five crackers and ask your auditory learner to touch the crackers that you indicate when you say the ordinal numbers. Eat the crackers for a snack.

Mastery occurs when: your child understands how ordinal numbers show a specific position.

You may want to help your child a little more if: he is having trouble with ordinal numbers. Start with two objects. Ask your child to put the two objects in a specific order. Ask him which one is first, then ask which one is second. Do this with two objects until your child is successful and then move up to three objects.

4 | That's an Order!

On each of the twelve index cards, write one of the following: "clap your hands," "jump up and down," "stomp your foot," "nod your head," "blink your eyes," "rub your tummy," "kick your foot," "point at me," "wiggle your body," "say a-ha," "wave hello," and "turn around."

TIME: 15 minutes

MATERIALS
■ 12 index cards
■ marker

Learning happens when: your child completes physical tasks in a specific order. Shuffle the cards and place them facedown. Ask your child to draw two cards. Read the cards to your child and ask her to do the two tasks in order. For example, if you draw the "clap" and "turn around" cards, ask your child to first clap her hands and then turn around. Continue until all the cards have been played.

Variations: When your child is comfortable with two tasks, draw three cards, and ask her to complete the three tasks in order.

✋ Teach your kinesthetic learner the song "Head, Shoulders, Knees, and Toes" and have her follow the sequence of movements in the song.

👁 Look through magazines with your visual learner to find pictures of things that must come in a certain order. Ask him to cut the pictures out (with safety scissors) and glue them on a paper across from each other in order (for example, baby and adult, seed and plant, bowl of batter and cake or cookie, wound and bandage, rain and puddle).

👂 Play a listening game with your auditory learner. Say to her, "Which comes first: 'Color this picture' or 'Get your crayons'? Why?" Continue the game (saying, for example, "Put toothpaste on your toothbrush" and "Brush your teeth"; "Get dressed" and "Get out of bed"; "Take your plate to the sink" and "Eat your dinner").

Mastery occurs when: your child can successfully complete the actions in order.

You may want to help your child a little more if: she is having difficulty completing the actions in order. Model the activity for your child. She will get a kick out of seeing you complete the actions.

5 Numeral Snakes

Prepare for this activity by writing the numerals 0–9 on the sheets of card stock. Use one numeral on each sheet. If you do not have cardboard or card stock, you can use wax paper and a permanent marker for writing the numerals.

Learning happens when: your child uses the clay to make different numerals. Give him one of the written numerals. Show him how to roll out snakes from the clay and ask him to use the written numeral as a guide to laying down the snake in the shape of the numeral. After your child has completed the numeral snake, ask him to trace the snake with his finger while saying the number. Repeat these steps until all the numbers have been traced.

Variations: Allow your child to practice writing the numeral after he has made the numeral snake. You may want to write the numeral first and ask your child to trace your numeral several times before writing it independently.

✌ Ask your kinesthetic learner to draw the numerals in a plate or small box that contains dry cornmeal or sand. He should look at the numeral carefully before he draws it. When he makes mistakes, he can just smooth the cornmeal and start again.

👁 Give your visual learner a number line that goes to 10, paper, numeral stamps, and a stamp pad. Ask him to match the numerals and make his own number line.

👂 With your auditory learner, read the book *Ten Black Dots,* by Donald Crews, and teach one of the rhymes to him. Ask him to count the dots on each page.

Mastery occurs when: your child can connect the number to its numeral.

TIME: 10 minutes

MATERIALS
- 10 sheets of $8\frac{1}{2} \times 11$-inch card stock (or any thick paper or cardboard)
- marker
- modeling clay

You may want to help your child a little more if: he is having difficulty with this task. Make sure your child's clay snakes are long enough. If he is having trouble manipulating the clay, assist him with making the snakes. Guide your child's hands when laying down the snakes. Do not complete the activity for him, but suggest where to start and the best path to take along the numeral.

6 | Numeral Match

TIME: 10 minutes

MATERIALS
- 20 index cards
- marker
- 45 small stickers (any shape)

Take ten of the index cards and use the marker to write one of the numerals 0–9 on each card. Also write the word name of each numeral. Your cards will look something like those in the figure.

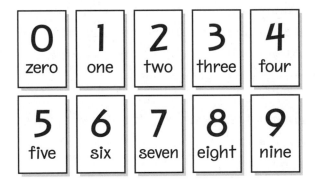

On the remaining ten index cards, use stickers to make matching cards (seven stickers to match the 7/seven card, for example).

Learning happens when: your child plays a game matching the number of objects on a card with its numeral. Lay out the numeral cards faceup in order. Shuffle the sticker cards and place them facedown in a pile on the table. Ask your child to draw a card and match the number of stickers on the card with its numeral. Continue until she has matched all the cards.

Variations: Try using the numeral cards and a cup of forty-five dried beans. Shuffle the cards. Ask your child to draw a numeral card and then put the appropriate number of dried beans on the card. Continue until she has used all the cards.

✋ For kinesthetic learners use the variation of the activity.

👁 Play a game of Concentration with your visual learner. Shuffle the cards and place all twenty cards down in a grid pattern. Each player turns over two cards, trying to match the sticker card with its numeral card. The player who makes the most matches wins the game.

👂 Play a game with your auditory learner. Write the numerals 1–5 on a sheet of paper, but leave one blank where a number should be written. Ask your child to tell you what number is left out. Expect her to count aloud each time you present a question. Continue as long as the game holds your child's interest.

Mastery occurs when: your child can successfully match the number of stickers with its numeral.

You may want to help your child a little more if: she is having trouble matching the numerals with the number of stickers. Start with the 0–5 numeral cards and the matching sticker cards. When your child is successful with these cards, add one or two more pairs. When your child can match the 0–7 cards, add the last two pairs. Soon your child will be recognizing numerals and knowing which number the numeral represents.

7 | Who Has More?

Time: 10 minutes

Materials
- 20 index cards
- marker

Prepare the twenty index cards in the following way: take five of the cards and draw one dot on the first card, two dots on the second card, three dots on the third card, four dots on the fourth card, and five dots on the fifth card. Draw the dots so they resemble the dots on a die. Make a total of four sets of five. In the end, your cards should look something like the ones in the figure.

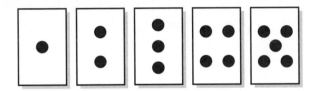

Learning happens when: your child plays a game that requires him to add by counting dots. Shuffle the cards and place them facedown in a pile between you and your child. Each player will draw two cards and count the total number of dots on both cards. The player with more dots takes all four cards. Continue playing in this way until all the cards have been played.

Variations: Once your child can easily do the activity, prepare sixteen more index cards in the same way, using six to nine dots per card. Add these to the original set and play the game again.

With your kinesthetic learner, play a similar game using dominoes; ask him to turn the dominoes over so that the dots don't show and mix them up. Take turns drawing one domino and compare the two, and whoever has more dots keeps both dominoes. Repeat until all the dominoes are played.

👁 Play a game with your visual learner. Prepare a number line showing the numerals 1–10. Players take turns rolling a die and placing a marker over that numeral on the number line. The player with the larger number gets to go first the next time.

👂 Read a counting book to your auditory learner (for example, *Over in the Meadow,* by Ezra Jack Keats; *Count and See,* by Tana Hoban; *Ten What? A Mystery Counting Book,* by Russell Hoban). Ask him to count the objects on the pages of the book.

Mastery occurs when: your child can successfully combine the dots on the two cards.

You may want to help your child a little more if: he is having trouble adding the dots. Ask your child to touch the dots as he counts. If necessary, guide his finger, touching each dot and modeling how to count the dots.

8 | Move 'em Out!

Learning happens when: you and your child play a game to be the first person to empty her cup. Each player gets a cup containing thirty small items. A bowl is placed between the players. The object of the game is to get rid of all the objects in the cup by putting them into the bowl. The number of items that each person can remove from her cup will be determined by the die. To begin, each player rolls the die, and the person with the higher number goes first. The first player rolls the die, removes that number of items from the cup, and puts the items into the bowl. Play then

TIME: 10 minutes

MATERIALS
▪ 2 paper cups
▪ plastic bowl
▪ 60 small items, such as dried lima beans, 30 in each cup
▪ die

goes to player two, who will roll the die and remove the appropriate number of items from her cup into the bowl. Play continues until one player removes her last item from the cup. That person is declared the winner.

Variations: You can play this activity at snack time, using the snack as the items in the cup. Instead of removing the items to the bowl, the players can eat that number of items. This would work well with small crackers, grapes, raisins, and the like.

For your kinesthetic learner, write the numerals 0–5 on paper muffin liners; place them in a muffin tin. Give your child a bowl of dry cereal and tell her that she should count the pieces of cereal to match the numbers in the muffin tin.

Read a counting book to your visual learner (for example: *Cookie Count,* by Robert Sabuda; *Anno's Counting House,* by Mitsumasa Anno; *1, 2, 3 Pop!* by Rachael Isadora; *Count,* by Denise Flemming). Be sure to let her count the items on the page.

Teach this finger play to your auditory learner. Use both hands as potatoes and use your fingers for counting.

One potato *(show one finger)*, two potato *(show two fingers)*, three potato *(show three fingers)*, four *(show four fingers)*!

Well, I made a batch of hot potatoes *(bend forward and stir as in a big pot)*

Dropped 'em on the floor! *(look shocked and put hands on face in surprise)*

Five potato *(show five fingers)*, six potato *(show six fingers)*, seven potato *(show seven fingers)*, eight *(show eight fingers)*!

So I stomped 'em into mashed potatoes *(stomp feet while walking forward a few steps and then back)*

And plopped 'em on a plate! *(pretend to put potatoes on a plate)*

Nine potato *(show nine fingers),* ten potato *(show ten fingers),* can't believe my eyes! *(cover and uncover eyes in surprise)*

The children ate 'em up and now they want some french fries! *(say to your child "How many?" and march with swinging arms and stomping feet while counting)*

1, 2, 3, 4, 5, 6, 7, 8, 9, 10 fries! *(jump up and reach over head to sky on 10)*

"Again??" *(do the count again faster and a third time even faster)*

Mastery occurs when: your child can determine the number represented by the die and count the appropriate number of items to remove from the cup.

You may want to help your child a little more if: she is having difficulty with some aspect of the activity. Your child may be having trouble determining the number represented by the die. Ask her to count the dots. If your child is having trouble removing the appropriate number of items, ask her to remove the appropriate number of items to the table first. Once she has done that, ask her to count the number of dots on the die and then the number of items on the table. If the numbers match, she can move the items to the bowl. If the numbers do not match, give your child the opportunity to fix it.

9 | Bead Patterns

TIME: 15 minutes

MATERIALS
- approximately 60 beads (30 of one color, 30 of another color)
- 4 strands of yarn (each approximately 12 inches long)

Prepare the patterns by tying a knot toward the bottom of each of the strands of yarn. Make sure the knots are large enough to keep the beads from slipping off the yarn. Take the first strand of yarn and string eight beads in an AB pattern (for example, red-blue-red-blue-red-blue-red-blue). Tie another knot so that the beads stay in place. Take the second strand of yarn and string eight beads in an AABB pattern (for example, red-red-blue-blue-red-red-blue-blue). Tie another knot to keep the beads in place. Take the third strand of yarn and string nine beads in an ABB pattern (for example, red-blue-blue-red-blue-blue-red-blue-blue). Tie a knot to keep the beads in place. Take the final strand of yarn and string nine beads in an AAB pattern (for example, red-red-blue-red-red-blue-red-red-blue). Tie a knot to keep the beads in place. Make sure there's plenty of yarn left so your child can string additional beads. The strands will look something like the illustration.

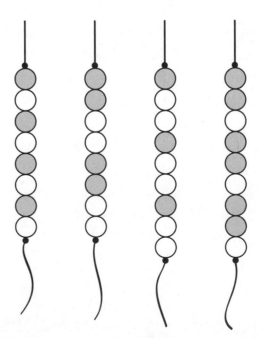

Learning happens when: your child identifies and extends patterns made with beads. Ask him to pick a strand and touch each bead in order while saying its color out loud. When your child has finished the strand, ask him to state the color that comes next. Once he understands the pattern, ask him to put more beads on the strand, following the pattern. Continue in the same way until your child can extend all four patterns.

Variations: Once your child is comfortable with this activity, introduce another color and ask him to create patterns with the three colors. He could then make a necklace or bracelet that highlights his favorite pattern.

✋ Sit with your kinesthetic learner and talk about AB patterns. Ask him to think of something that he can do to make a pattern and then have him build an AB pattern using those movements (for example, clap and stomp, clap and roll hands in circle, or sit and stand).

👁 Visual learners will see the pattern a little faster than children with other learning styles and should be able to use the beads to make at least two different AB patterns. You should then begin another pattern—remembering to make it long enough to repeat itself one time—and ask your child to name and finish making the pattern.

👂 Auditory learners can "read" the patterns aloud and tell you what should go next in the pattern or "read" his own patterns to check for accuracy.

Mastery occurs when: your child identifies and extends each pattern.

You may want to help your child a little more if: he is having difficulty identifying and continuing the patterns. Ask your child to lay the strand down on the table. Next, ask him to put down beads to copy the pattern beside the strand. Once the pattern is laid down, ask your child to pick up the strand and string the beads on the strand in the order in which they are laid on the table.

10 Money Sort

TIME: 10 minutes

MATERIALS
- assorted coins (pennies, nickels, dimes, and quarters)
- 4 plastic bowls

Learning happens when: your child sorts a handful of coins. Give her the coins and ask her to separate them: all the pennies in one bowl, the nickels in another, and so on. If your child is competitive, get a stopwatch to see how fast she can complete the task.

Variations: To extend this activity once the coins are sorted, ask your child to count the number of coins in each of the bowls to see which bowl has the most. Your child can also make a train of each type of coin and then compare the trains. Which type of coin makes the longest train? Which type of coin makes the shortest train?

✋ Go to your kinesthetic learner's room with her and begin by talking about the coin sorting activity. Say "Can you think of any way we can sort your toys?" You may need to begin the game by asking, "Do you have toys that are soft? You can sort your toys into soft and not-soft groups."

👁 Give your visual learner an assortment of uncooked pasta in a variety of shapes. Ask her to sort the pasta into groups that look the same.

👂 For your auditory learner, cut pictures of fruit from magazines and give them to her, allow time for her to name the fruits, then say, "Can you think of a way to sort the fruit and then explain it to me?" (Some examples might include sorting by color, by like or dislike, or by size.)

Mastery occurs when: your child can successfully separate the different types of coins.

You may want to help your child a little more if: she is having trouble telling the coins apart. The pennies will be easiest to distinguish because of their color. Nickels, dimes, and quarters may be more difficult for your child. Take time to really look at the coins. Help your child notice the pictures on them. Point out that the nickel has a smooth edge, whereas the quarters and dimes have a serrated edge. Notice the size of the coins. Allow your child to work with coins as much as possible, and she will learn to distinguish them quickly.

11 Does It Fit?

TIME: 20 minutes

MATERIALS
- old magazines
- safety scissors
- glue
- construction paper
- marker

Learning happens when: your child searches for items that fit within a given category. Give your child a basic category, such as red things, fast things, big things, soft things, or wet things. Take a sheet of construction paper and write the category at the top of the page. Talk to your child about the category and brainstorm with him about things that could fit in the category. After speaking with your child, give him the old magazines and ask him to find and cut out pictures of things that fit in the category. Once he has found several things that fit, ask him to glue them to the sheet of paper. Continue with other categories.

Variations: If your child really enjoys this activity, ask him to create collages for several categories, and make a book of your child's work.

✌ Ask your kinesthetic learner to help you take the laundry from the dryer and get the clothes that belong to him while you get the rest of the laundry and begin to fold it. Ask how to categorize what you've just done. Ask if he can name the other categories that you make as you fold the clothes together. Examples of possible categories are clothes folded for Mom, Dad, and child—or towels, sheets, play clothes, and pajamas.

👁 Explain to your visual learner that when you put away the groceries, you categorize the cans and boxes in different places in the cabinet. Ask your child to put away the unbreakable groceries according to the categories that he sees in the cabinet.

👂 Before you begin, go through old catalogues and cut out pictures of clothing that is seasonal—some for summer, some for winter. Talk with your auditory learner about the day's weather and how the clothes we wear are different in different seasons. Talk about what he wears in the summer that he would never wear in the winter, and vice versa. Give your child the pictures of clothing and ask him to sort them into two groups: winter clothing and summer clothing. Let him explain his choices when he's finished.

Mastery occurs when: your child can find items that fit within a given category.

You may want to help your child a little more if: he is having difficulty finding items that fit. Make sure your category is not too abstract. Start with a simple category, such as things that are a particular color, or people. If your child is still having trouble, sit down with him and look through the magazines together. Discuss the things you find and determine whether they fit or not. Once you find a few pictures with your child, ask him to try to find one more thing that fits. Soon your child will be able to do this activity independently.

Geometry and Measurement

Mention the word "geometry" and many adults find themselves reliving painful memories of proofs and theorems from high school math. Though most people think of geometry at the high school level, they may not realize that children explore geometry at the very start of their educational careers. Preschoolers are not proving theorems, but they are exploring the concepts of shape, relative position, and perspective.

Preschoolers will be exploring shapes, including triangles, squares, rectangles, and circles. They will be learning about how each shape is different from others. In addition to studying shapes, preschoolers will explore relative position and perspective. They will learn to use such words as "to the right of," "to the left of," "between," "beside," "above," and "below" to describe the position of an object. They will also look at how a figure may appear different as the viewer's perspective changes.

In addition to geometry, your child will begin exploring measurement. Preschoolers compare objects and put them in order according to size. They may start with two objects and tell which is larger and then move on to three objects, putting them in order from shortest to tallest. Your preschooler will also explore measuring time. She will be learning the days of the week and the months of the year. She will be looking at a calendar daily and will explore the past, present, and future by looking at yesterday, today, and tomorrow. Finally, your child will begin using nonstandard units to measure objects. Measuring with a nonstandard unit is using any item that is not specifically designed for measurement. For example, your child may make a train of crayons to see how long a box is. If he makes a train of five crayons across a box, he would say that the box is five crayons long. Your child will not begin to use measurement tools, such as rulers, until a later age.

Geometry and Measurement Skills	Having Problems?	Quick Tips
Recognizes two-dimensional shapes, such as circles, squares, rectangles, and triangles	Cannot differentiate between shapes	Help your child find these shapes in his environment. Ask your child to name the shape of a door, a window, or a clock face. Helping your child notice shapes in his environment will help him learn the shapes very quickly.
Tells the relative position of an object, using such words as "above," "below," "beside," "on," "next to," "to the right of," and "to the left of"	Has trouble describing the position of an object	Use these descriptive words as much as possible in everyday conversation. Ask your child to put the plate *on* the counter, slide the box *under* the bed, or set the book *next to* the vase. Ask her to describe where an object is, using these words. With practice, your child will quickly learn to describe an object's position.
Compares and orders objects	Has trouble comparing objects	This is another skill that can be developed with informal practice. Ask your child to compare things. Which is bigger—a grape or a lemon? A lion or a mouse? A tree or a flower? Grab a few spoons of different sizes and ask your child to point to the largest spoon and to the smallest spoon. Then ask him to put them in order from smallest to largest or largest to smallest. The key is to get your child to start noticing differences in size.
Knows the days of the week and the months of the year	Does not know the days of the week or the months of the year	Help your child develop this skill by posting a large calendar in a central place. Look at the calendar with your child every day. Point to today's date. Point out upcoming events and count how many days away the event is. Your child will learn about the days of the week very quickly if she can see a calendar every day.
Measures items using non-standard units	Has trouble measuring items	This skill is introduced and practiced but not necessarily mastered in preschool. If your child likes to make trains of items, ask her to see how many items need to be in a train that goes across a table or is as long as her foot. The items can be anything—paper clips, toy cars, blocks. The idea is to expose your child to how measuring works.

Geometry and Measurement Activities

1 Shape Hunt

Draw a circle at the top of the first sheet of construction paper, a square at the top of the second sheet, a rectangle at the top of the third sheet, and a triangle at the top of the fourth.

Learning happens when: your child searches for different shapes in old magazines. Ask your child to go through the magazines and find samples of all four shapes. Once he has found a shape, ask him to cut it out and glue it to the appropriate sheet of paper. Continue until there are several examples of each shape.

Variations: Your child can make a mini–shape book. Stack three or four sheets of construction paper on top of each other, fold them in half, and staple along the fold. Ask your child to pick some of his favorite shapes that have been cut out. Glue one shape on each page. Ask your child to tell you what each object is and write it down for him on the corresponding page.

Kinesthetic learners should explore attribute blocks (or cardboard models) and be allowed to play with them for a while before you begin to ask questions. (Attribute blocks are small wooden shapes, and usually all the blocks of the same shape are painted the same color.) They are great for building designs and patterns. Ask your child to pick up a square, circle, triangle, and rectangle; praise his responses. Talk with him as he builds something using the blocks, reminding him of the names of the shapes as needed.

For your visual learner, cut five to ten of each of the four main shapes (circle, square, rectangle, and triangle) from colored

TIME: 10 minutes

MATERIALS
- old magazines
- safety scissors
- glue
- 4 sheets of construction paper
- marker

construction paper. Give your child these pieces and a large sheet of paper. Ask him to make a design on the paper using the shapes. When you view the design, admire it and then ask "What is this shape?" as you touch different parts of the design. Help your child glue the shapes onto the paper, and hang it as artwork.

☞ Read your auditory learner a book about shapes (for example, *Circus Shapes,* by Stuart J. Murphy; *What Is Square?* and *What Is Round?* by Rebecca Kai Dotlich; *So Many Circles, So Many Squares,* by Tana Hoban).

Mastery occurs when: your child can find several different examples of the various shapes.

You may want to help your child a little more if: he is having trouble finding the shapes. Make sure your child searches for one shape at a time. Pick a shape and ask him to look only for that shape. When he has found four or five examples, ask him to glue it onto the sheet of construction paper. Once your child has completed one shape, move on to the next one. If he needs more help, try searching with him and guiding him to three or four shapes. Ask your child to find one more, while you casually withdraw from the process.

2 Shape Slap

TIME: 10 minutes

MATERIALS
- 4 paper plates
- marker
- clean flyswatter

Prepare for the activity by drawing a circle on one paper plate, a square on another paper plate, a rectangle on the third paper plate, and a triangle on the fourth.

Learning happens when: your child plays a game identifying various shapes. Lay the paper plates on the table. Give your child the flyswatter and tell her that you will be calling out different shapes. Your child will use the flyswatter to slap the plate that has the shape on it. Randomly call out the shapes and let your child slap the shape. As she becomes more proficient, quicken the pace of the game.

Variations: Once your child can easily slap the given shapes, tell her you will be calling out different items. Ask her to think about the item and slap the shape that best fits the items. The following are some examples:

Circle: CD, clock face, plate, quarter, ball, M&Ms

Rectangle: shoe box, ruler, door, window, magazine, envelope

Square: postage stamp, tile, Polaroid picture

Triangle: tortilla chips, crackers, slice of pizza

Note: some individual items may fit in more than one shape category—for example, a pillow may be round, square, or rectangular. Use items you have around the house and things with which your child is familiar.

Give your kinesthetic learner an assortment of crackers to sort by shape. Be sure to include more than two shapes of crackers (saltines are usually square, Ritz crackers are round, and so on). Ask your child to name the shapes.

With your visual learner, read books about shapes (for example, *Round and Round and Round,* by Tana Hoban; *Shapes,* by Keith Faulkner; *Shapes,* by Karen Gundersheimer), and as you do so, ask her to find different shapes within the pictures.

Before you begin, cut shapes from different colored construction paper. Lay the shapes on the table in front of your child. Relate the attributes of the shapes by asking your auditory learner to pick up the shape you name and answer questions about the shape (for example, "Does it have a corner?" "Is it green?" "Does it have two sides?" "How many sides does it have?")

Mastery occurs when: your child can connect the name of the shape with a picture of the shape.

You may want to help your child a little more if: she is having trouble identifying the shapes. Start with two simple shapes, such as a circle and square. Play with two shapes until your child can readily identify them. Once your child is successful with two shapes, introduce another one.

3 Cold, Warm, Hot!

TIME: 5 minutes

MATERIALS
▪ small item

Learning happens when: your child uses descriptive words to describe the location of a hidden object. This is an extension of a game you probably played as a child. Send your child out of the room and hide a small object. Call him back into the room and help him find the object by saying "cold" when he is far from the object, "warm" when he is near the object, and "hot" when he is close enough to touch the object. The most important part of the activity is for your child to tell you where the object was, using such words as "under," "on top of," "beside," and the like. If the object was under the pillow, for example, your child would say, "It was under the pillow."

Variations: Let your child hide the object and call out "cold," "warm," and "hot" as you try to find it. Upon finding the object, ask your child to describe where he hid the object, using the position words.

✌ Ask your kinesthetic learner to put himself in the position that you say (for example, "Put your whole body under the table," "Put your arm over the sink," "Put your whole body in a chair," "Walk through the doorway," "Stand beside the sofa"). Give your child a turn to choose a place to move, and you guess the position.

👁 Sit down with your visual learner and look at family photographs; ask him to touch the things that are in the positions you describe. You might ask him to point to the person in front of Grandpa or ask whether the person beside you is inside the house or outside.

👂 Give your auditory learner a small block. Tell him to listen to what you say and then to repeat what you said as he puts the block in that position (for example, "Put the block under the chair [over your head, behind you, into the drawer, between you and me]"). Correct any mistakes gently.

Mastery occurs when: your child can describe the position of the hidden object relative to other items.

You may want to help your child a little more if: he is having trouble describing the position of the object. Use questions to help him clarify the position. For example, if your child found the object but cannot describe its position, ask him, "What was the item behind?" Your child may answer, "The plant." You then affirm his answer and restate it in the words you would like your child to use, such as "That's right! The item was behind the plant."

4 | Tangram Twins

TIME: 10 minutes

MATERIALS
■ 2 tangrams

Note: a tangram has seven separate pieces. The shapes of the pieces are specially designed to fit together in a certain way. Tangram pieces are used to create different pictures, depending on how they are turned and fit together. Tangrams can be found in educational stores. If you cannot find them, you can use the printable version on the Internet at www.knowledgeessentials.com.

Learning happens when: your child replicates the tangram design you put together with your set. Use three or four tangram pieces to create a design. Ask your child to use her tangram pieces to make a copy of the design you have created. As your child gets more comfortable, use more pieces to make a larger design or make your design more complex.

Variations: Ask your child to use one complete tangram to create a picture or design. Then give her the second tangram and ask her to make a copy of the design she just made.

✋ Create a tangram pattern for your kinesthetic learner. Build a design using the tangram pieces and trace around the pieces as you remove them, leaving a design pattern on the paper. Explain to your child that this is a pattern for the design and that she needs to find the pieces that fit on the paper and to put them in the right places.

👁 For your visual learner, model building a design and allow her to reproduce it. Then ask her to do the variation activity.

👂 Begin to build a design as your child watches, talk about where you are placing the tangram pieces (using "above," "below," "beside," and "between" to describe). Ask your child to copy the design (you may need to start it for her). Continue until she tires of the activity. Repeat it several more times on other days.

Mastery occurs when: your child can replicate a design.

You may want to help your child a little more if: she is having difficulty copying the design. Start with very simple designs using even as few as two pieces. When your child can successfully duplicate simple designs, make them a little harder. Continue in this way to build your child's skill and confidence.

5 Order Up!

The first step is to prepare the index cards. Take the first five cards. Draw a circle on each card; however, the circles need to be obviously different sizes—extra small, small, medium, large, and extra large. Take the next five cards and draw five different sizes of triangles on them. Draw five different sizes of squares on the last five cards.

Learning happens when: your child organizes a group of cards by the size of the object drawn on it. Shuffle the cards and give them to your child. Ask him to separate the cards into a different pile for each shape. Once he has sorted the cards, he should organize each pile from smallest to largest.

Variations: Tell your child that *you* are going to play the game now. Give him five blank index cards. Ask him to create a set using the shape of his choosing—one extra-small, small, medium, large, and extra-large card. Then you get to put them in order. Of course, the purpose of this isn't to see whether you can do the activity correctly, but to check and see if your child was able to create the cards. You may also want to make a mistake to see if your child catches it.

TIME: 10 minutes

MATERIALS
- 15 index cards
- marker

👋 For an introduction to the lesson, ask your kinesthetic learner to place stuffed animals (or other toys) in order according to their size.

👁 Visual learners should do the variation of this activity.

👂 For your auditory learner, cut three shapes of different sizes from construction paper and ask him to put them in order from largest to smallest and vice versa. He should then describe the shapes and their sizes.

Mastery occurs when: your child can sort the cards and arrange them in order from smallest to largest.

You may want to help your child a little more if: he is having trouble sorting or arranging the cards. If your child is having trouble sorting, ask him to color-code the shapes first with markers or crayons. Once the cards are color-coded, your child should have no trouble sorting the cards. If the problem is in ordering the cards by size, ask him to pull out the largest and smallest shapes. Then ask him to order the remaining three cards. Once the three cards are ordered, he can place the largest and smallest on the ends.

6 Search and Order

Time: 20 minutes

Materials
- old magazines
- safety scissors
- glue
- paper

Learning happens when: your child finds three different sizes of the same object in old magazines. There are several kinds of images that appear frequently in magazines. For example, there are always pictures of people, cars, and houses in advertisements. Ask your child to find three different pictures of people. The pictures need to be different sizes—one small, one medium, and one large. Ask your child to glue the pictures in order from smallest to largest or largest to smallest.

Variations: If finding the different sizes is too easy for your child, ask her to find three pictures of people at different ages (such as baby, child, and adult) or of things that move, ranking from slowest to fastest (for example, turtle, person, and horse) There really is no limit to things that can be ordered.

Kinesthetic learners need to arrange real things in order first. You can ask your child to arrange items from the pantry in order of their size.

Read your visual learner a book about size (for example, *Bigger and Smaller,* by Robert Froman; *Big Ones, Little Ones* and *Is It Larger? Is It Smaller?* by Tana Hoban) and ask her to identify the sizes in the illustrations.

Tell your auditory learner the story of Goldilocks and the Three Bears, stressing sizes when you describe the things belonging to Papa, Mama, and Baby Bear. Ask questions about the story afterwards—for example, "Who did the biggest bed belong to?" and "Can you tell me which bowl belonged to Baby Bear?"

Mastery occurs when: your child can find three different sizes of things and can place them in order.

You may want to help your child a little more if: she has trouble finding the objects. Find and cut out the pictures yourself and ask your child to put them in order and glue them to the paper.

7 | The Long and Short of It

TIME: 20 minutes

MATERIALS
- medium-size box
- several objects of different sizes (some larger than the box, some small enough to fit inside it)

Learning happens when: you give your child the box and have him look at the size of it and then find three items that can be placed in it. Tell your child that the box has to stay on the table. This requires him to estimate and use spatial reasoning to determine if each object will actually fit inside the box. Encourage your child not to choose only very small items.

Variations: Use a small, medium, and large box for this activity.

- Your kinesthetic learner will enjoy the variation of this activity.

- Show your visual learner how to measure the box with his hands and then to use this measure to help him estimate whether an object will fit inside the box.

- Auditory learners can go on a modified version of a treasure hunt in which you give him directions or clues to find something that will fit in the box.

Mastery occurs when: your child can compare objects and can guess which ones will fit into the box.

You may want to help your child a little more if: he is having difficulty managing the task. If the task is overwhelming, narrow it down a bit. Ask your child to find one of his toys that will fit in the box.

8 How Many Paper Clips?

Learning happens when: your child uses the nonstandard unit of paper clips to measure various items. Take one of the items and ask your child to see how many paper clips it takes to make a train as long as the item. Make sure your child understands that the ends of the paper clips must touch but cannot overlap. Once she has created a train of paper clips the same length as the object, ask her to state the object's measurement in paper clips. If it takes a train of seven paper clips to equal the length of a calculator, your child would say, "The calculator is seven paper clips long." Continue in the same way for the other objects. Most objects will not be measured exactly in paper clips. The idea is to find approximately how many paper clips it takes, so expect your child to be close, not exact.

Variations: If your child finds this to be easy, introduce a ruler and show her which lines go with the numbers. Teach your child to line up the edge of the object being measured with the edge of the ruler. Your child will enjoy using a "grown-up" tool to measure objects.

TIME: 10 minutes

MATERIALS
- box of paper clips
- various items to be measured

Kinesthetic learners should experiment with different non-standard units in measuring objects. For example, she could try measuring with building blocks, pencils laid end to end, and Popsicle sticks.

Give your visual learner a bag that contains different things for her to measure using the train of paper clips. After she has measured them, ask her to line the objects up in order of their size from longest to shortest.

👂 Auditory learners should follow your oral directions in doing the following activity. Tell her that you will use string to help her measure different parts of her body—for example, the arm from elbow to wrist, the length of your foot, the leg from knee to ankle. Have your child hold one end of the string while you hold the other, mark the string with a marker, and then cut it. Let your child compare the strings and describe the experience.

Mastery occurs when: your child understands how to use a nonstandard unit of measurement, such as paper clips, to measure an object.

You may want to help your child a little more if: she is having difficulty using the paper clips as a measurement tool. Most children understand the concept of making a train of items, as they may have been doing it at a young age. Try asking your child to make a train of paper clips without a specific object to be measured. Then take an object and line it up with the train. Remove any paper clips that extend beyond the edge of the object. Ask your child to count the remaining paper clips to complete the measurement.

9 | Calendar Time at Home

Learning happens when: you and your child work with the calendar daily. Post a large calendar in an accessible area. Each day look at the calendar with your child. Say the day and full date with him. For example, "Today is Saturday, May 13, 2006." Talk about what day it was yesterday and what day it will be tomorrow. Talk about any events that are coming up on the calendar. Count how many days away the next event is. Finally, at the end of the day, allow your child to mark an **X** on the calendar for the day that is done.

Variations: Talk about the order of the days of the week and show the column on the calendar of each of the days of the week. Say the names of the days, stress the beginning sound, then point to

TIME: 5 minutes

MATERIALS
▪ large calendar
▪ marker

the word on the calendar. Point out that the numbers move from left to right in rows. Talk about and show how rows and columns are different.

🖐 Kinesthetic learners should do the variation activity; they can touch the calendar and trace with their finger the rows and columns (you may need to model this for them). They should also touch the numbers on the calendar as they count to find the date.

👁 Your visual learner should write an **X** on the calendar to mark the day's date over a period of several months. You should point to the name of the month and day as you talk about the date each day. Say the date and ask your child to repeat it.

👂 Teach your auditory learner to sing this song about the days of the week (sung to the tune of the *Addams Family* theme song):

> There's Sunday and there's Monday,
> There's Tuesday and there's Wednesday,
> There's Thursday and there's Friday,
> And then there's Saturday.
> Days of the week *(clap, clap)*
> Days of the week *(clap, clap)*
> Days of the week, days of the week, days of the week *(clap, clap)*

Mastery occurs when: your child understands the basic organization of a calendar and knows the days of the week.

You may want to help your child a little more if: he is having difficulty with this daily routine. Your child will probably struggle with it at first. He may forget the days of the week, not know the numbers on the calendar, and so on. Be persistent. It may take several weeks, but if this is a routine, your child will catch on.

Environmental Learning

Math for your preschooler will be exploratory in nature. Preschool is a time of introduction, when children are exposed to new concepts. She will not be expected to master every skill. You can continue this process by talking about numbers and shapes in daily life. "I need two apples from the refrigerator. One, two." "I have three cookies, I have two cookies, I have one cookie." "I like the notebook with the red circle on it." "We will eat four ears of corn at dinner. One, two, three, four. One for you, one for Dad, one for Sally, and one for me. That's four."

Your child has many years of math education ahead of him. As he participates in these kinds of activities, he is laying a strong foundation, developing number sense, and will be prepared to meet future mathematical challenges.

End of Preschool Math Checklist

Students who are working at the standard level at the end of preschool:

____ Will recognize some numerals

____ Count orally to five

____ Recognize shapes—circle, square, triangle, rectangle

____ Compare, describe, and order objects by size

____ Compare sets of objects and describe them as "more" or "less"

____ Measure objects using informal measurement

____ Begin to understand some time concepts (yesterday, today, tomorrow)

Preschool Science 8

I'm sure you've noticed your child touching and examining everything around her. A four-year-old child is naturally curious and is constantly learning about her environment. As a result, the preschool student will be more than ready to learn science concepts. Make it fun—not only will she remember it, but you'll also help keep her interested in science as she gets older.

Science for four-year-olds includes things they see in their everyday environment at home, outside, and in their neighborhoods. In fact, your child has probably already been exploring the scientific process. Is "Why?" your child's most frequent question? It can be exhausting answering a string of "why" questions, but your child is developing an important skill in science: the ability to ask questions and to wonder about things. You don't have to know all the answers to every question. It's perfectly acceptable to say things like "I'm not sure," "Let's see," "What do you think?" or "Let's try this or that." In fact, it's important to ask your child questions and to try to make science fun.

Encourage your child to make observations about everything he sees and be sure to talk to your child about what he sees so that he makes a connection with the observation. It is important for children to feel connected to the experience in order for it to be meaningful, so be sure to relate what he is seeing to something else that he knows about. Your child will also be comparing objects and describing what they have in common or how they are different, called grouping or classification, another skill used in the scientific process.

Four-year-old children are exposed to dozens of scientific opportunities in their everyday environment. Ask your child questions about earth materials while she is playing in the water at bath time or playing in the sand or dirt.

Science is divided into two broad categories—science processes and science concepts. Science processes include these activities:

- Playing with objects to discover information
- Asking questions and making observations
- Describing objects according to what they have in common or the ways they are different

Science concepts for four-years-olds are taught in the areas of physical science, life science, and earth and space science.

Physical science concepts include these activities:

- Using the five senses
- Comparing objects

Life science concepts include these activities:

- Examining whether something is a living or nonliving thing
- Learning about what plants and animals need in order to grow

Earth and space science concepts include these activities:

- Learning about the properties of common earth materials, such as soil, water, and rocks
- Observing and describing the daily weather and the four seasons

Science Processes

Teaching science to preschoolers requires that it be fun and exploratory in nature. Science processes skills for preschool should include observation, classification, and communication. Making observations of things in the child's environment is the most natural place to start; be a weather watcher and talk about your observations, notice the different kinds of clouds and the different colors, and discuss the way the weather feels (hot, cool, wet, windy, and so on).

Science Processes Skills	Having Problems?	Quick Tips
Uses the five senses to identify and describe objects	Uses only visual clues to describe objects	Talk about objects with which your child is familiar, using words that describe the objects' feel, taste, and smell and the sounds they make. Point out the most obvious similarities and differences in the objects.
Conducts simple experiments	Would rather play	Approach all activities as play in order to capture your child's attention to learn. All learning is based on some former knowledge about the subject. Let your child guide you in the direction that interests him. Ask him leading questions that will promote further experimentation.
Talks about observations	Says "I don't know" or has nothing to say	Ask questions about the activity as you are doing it. Later, let your child call a relative or friend to tell that person what she did.

Science Processes Activities

1 Sink or Float?

TIME: 10 minutes

MATERIALS
- bucket or pan full of water
- variety of small objects (for example, paper clip, sponge, marble, toys, cork)
- two paper plates
- paper towels
- marker

Learning happens when: you ask your child to perform an experiment. Draw a simple picture of a boat on one plate. Explain to your child that a boat floats, so any item that floats will go on that plate. Draw a picture of an anchor on the other paper plate. Explain to your child that an anchor sinks, so any item that sinks will go on that plate. Line up the objects and ask him if he thinks each object will sink or float. Test your child's predictions by having him place the objects one at a time into the bucket or pan full of water. After testing each item, dry it with a paper towel and place it on the correct plate.

Variations: Ask questions and make suggestions as your child performs the experiment. Can you make something that sinks float? Try putting a sinking object on a floating object. Which object sinks fastest? How many objects will a sponge hold before it sinks? Let your child play with this experiment by trying out different variations.

✋ Your kinesthetic learner will want to try many different objects in the water and talk about them all. Let him help you gather more objects for the experiment. Talk to him about the weight of each item.

👁 Ask your visual learner what will happen if you mix oil with water. Begin by putting water in a clear plastic bottle and let your child put some blue food coloring into the water. Put the cap on the bottle and shake it up. What happens? Now add a spoonful of cooking oil to the mixture and shake to mix. What happens?

🜋 Ask your auditory learner to report on the experiment by telling you what he did. Write down his words. Afterwards, read what you have written and ask your child if anything needs to be added or changed.

Mastery occurs when: your child can explain "sink" and "float" and can recall some of the objects that sink and some that float.

You may want to help your child a little more if: he wants to play instead of sorting the objects and answering questions. This happens often with very young children. Give your child plenty of time for free play with water. You may need to come back to the activity several times.

2 Shadows

Learning happens when: you talk about shadows with your child. On a sunny day, go outside at different times of the day and find a place for your child to stand so that she sees her shadow. Make sure your child stands in the same spot each time. Mark the height of the shadow with the chalk so that your child can see the shadow grow and then shrink. Discuss the changes in the height of the shadow. Point out that the earth moves throughout the day and the changing angle of the sun is what changes the height of the shadows.

TIME: 5 minutes

MATERIALS
▪ sidewalk chalk

Variations: Pick a stationary object in your yard or another outdoor space to observe every day over a period of several weeks. Ask your child to make observations; be sure you call attention to the size and placement of the shadow on different days.

🖐 Ask your kinesthetic learner to pick two or three toys (that can stand alone) to place near the sidewalk for the day. Use sidewalk chalk to mark changes in the height of the shadows throughout the day. Compare the marks and talk about the changes.

👁 Use a flashlight and one of your visual learner's toys that can stand alone. In a darkened room, move the flashlight around as you shine it on the object, and observe the way the shadow changes.

👂 Ask your auditory learner to describe the experiment during dinner with the family, including details about the changes in the shadow.

Mastery occurs when: your child notices the changes in shadows and begins to relate some of the changes to light movement.

You may want to help your child a little more if: she finds the concept too difficult. Don't push it. Instead enjoy the observations and the wonder of it all. Four-year-olds won't understand all the concepts, and this is okay. What's important is that you've introduced your child to making the observations. The seed of curiosity has been planted, and your child will eventually begin to notice the changes in different places.

3 Exploring Color

TIME: 10 minutes

MATERIALS
- 5 or 6 clear glasses
- food coloring
- dropper
- sticky notes

Learning happens when: your child observes that there are many shades of the same color. Let your child see you measure the same amount of water into each glass, and ask him to choose a color of food coloring. Explain that he should use the dropper to put the food coloring into the water in the first glass and count the number of drops he puts in. Write the number on a sticky note and put it in front of the glass. Add more drops to each successive glass, thus creating different shades of the color. Talk about the changes in the color. Ask your child to explain how the changes happened.

Variations: Put shaving cream in zipper-style plastic bags. Drop the food coloring into the bags, close them, and ask your child to squeeze the bags gently to mix the color. Compare the shades of the color and the number of drops put into each bag.

✋ Your kinesthetic learner will love the variation of this activity.

👁 Set up cups, baby food jars, bowls, or other containers with small amounts of white paint. Add a small amount of one of your visual learner's favorite colors to each container of white. Talk to your child about how it looks when the color first hits the white and then how it looks when the colors are mixed. Ask your child to paint using the different shades. You'll need a paintbrush for each separate shade. Don't be surprised if your child covers the entire paper with the paint, as this is a common behavior at four years.

👂 Ask your auditory learner to explain the process of changing the shades of the color.

Mastery occurs when: your child begins to describe the observable changes in the water and associates the cause of the changes with the addition of food coloring.

You may want to help your child a little more if: he has problems seeing the different shades. Increase the amount of food color that you use and repeat the process. Use each of the suggested activities with your child.

4 | Wind

TIME: 10 minutes

MATERIALS

- crepe paper streamer
- cardboard tube (from wrapping paper, waxed paper, or aluminum foil)
- transparent tape

Learning happens when: you talk with your child about the wind and how we know when it's windy. Ask your child if she can see the wind. Give your child three or four paper streamers about two feet long and the paper tube. Help her tape the streamers onto the tube. Go outside together and experiment with moving the streamers as she waves the tube, walks, runs, or twirls. Ask your child to explain the movement.

Variations: Help your child recall experiences she has had with the wind (for example, hair blowing into her face, chasing some object that is being blown by the wind, watching the trees sway in the wind). Read a book about the wind to your child (for example, *The Wind Blew,* by Pat Hutchins, or *Please, Wind?* by Carol Greene).

✍ Let your kinesthetic learner experiment with moving different lengths of streamers and ask her to describe the differences.

👁 Go for a walk outside with your visual learner and look for objects that provide evidence that the wind is blowing, such as flags flapping, leaves swirling, hair moving, or clouds moving.

👂 Talk with your auditory learner about the sounds that wind makes. Ask her to make sounds like ones she has heard from the wind.

Mastery occurs when: your child can identify and explain some of the properties of wind.

You may want to help your child a little more if: she cannot tell you about the wind. Use each of the previously suggested activities with your child. Talk about the wind in your daily activities.

Physical Science

Your child will be using the five senses—sight, hearing, taste, smell, and touch—to describe and group objects. She may describe how something smells or the way it feels. Your child will explore grouping objects by looking for similarities and differences. Grouping will rely heavily on visual clues, but your child will learn to separate according to the other senses as well. For example, she may listen to various sounds and distinguish whether the sounds are loud or soft. In describing an object, your child will rely on language and vocabulary development. There will be times when you need to introduce words in order to reinforce vocabulary development with your four-year-old.

Physical Science Skills	Having Problems?	Quick Tips
Uses several attributes to describe an object	Does not include enough detail in descriptions	Try asking your child leading questions about the object. For example, "Is it hard or soft? big or little? red or yellow?"
Groups and explains the grouping	Wants to group everything as big or little	Try giving directions that include specific ways to group things differently.
Can describe similarities and differences	Has problems finding similarities and differences	Sort various objects with your child and describe the differences and similarities as you do so. Ask your child to join you and take turns looking for things that are similar or different.
Uses the five senses to experience and describe objects	Relies only on sight to describe objects	Direct your child in a game by asking him to use all the five senses to group objects. Gather some objects together and ask him to put, for example, all smooth things here and rough things there, or salty things here and sweet things there, heavy things here and light things there. This can be an ongoing activity.

Physical Science Activities

1 Magnifying Glasses

TIME: 10 minutes

MATERIALS
▪ handheld magnifying glass
▪ strawberries
▪ knife

Learning happens when: your child learns about using a magnifying glass to look at things that are very small. Give your child a strawberry (or any berry that is available) to look at with the magnifying glass. Ask him to look at the leaves too. Cut the strawberry in half and look at the inside. Ask your child to describe what he sees. Ask your child to smell the strawberry and then eat it. Then ask what it smells and taste like.

Variations: Use a flower or leaves from various plants and follow the activity described.

✋ Ask your kinesthetic learner to prepare more berries for a snack or a dessert that day by removing the leaves, washing them, and then putting them in a bowl.

👁 Cut a strawberry in half for your visual learner and let him make strawberry prints on white paper.

👂 Ask your auditory learner to describe the process of examining the strawberry, and his findings.

Mastery occurs when: your child discovers something that he did not know about strawberries and when he describes the way it smells, tastes, feels, and looks.

You may want to help your child a little more if: he is not interested in looking at the fruit. Look for something else that interests him more. You may want to take the magnifying glass outside and check out soil, tree bark, small insects, and so on. If your child has trouble describing his observations, ask leading questions that will help him recall and state the observations.

2 | Texture

Learning happens when: your child feels the textured objects in the gift bag. Talk with your child about the sense of touch and explain that texture is the way objects feel. Ask her to reach into the bag and pick up one thing. Before she pulls it out of the bag, ask your child to touch the object and describe the way it feels. Now ask your child to look at the object and describe the way it looks. You may need to supply some adjectives.

Variations: Take a walk outside and look for textures (for example, tree bark, the sidewalk, a mailbox, the door to your house, rocks), touch them, and describe them.

✍ Ask your kinesthetic learner to gather some things to put into the bag. Take turns playing the game again. Try to use a variety of adjectives when you play to introduce your child to new words.

👁 Play a game of I Spy with your visual learner, but be sure to include descriptions of both the texture and appearance of objects in the room.

👂 Throughout the rest of the day, ask your auditory learner to describe the way various things feel.

Mastery occurs when: your child can explain the sense of touch and begins to use more adjectives to describe objects.

You may want to help your child a little more if: she doesn't know enough words to use for describing objects. Model using different adjectives when doing the activity and be sure to use as many descriptive words as possible in front of your child every day.

TIME: 10 minutes

MATERIALS
- gift bag
- collection of things that have various textures (for example, orange, apple, and marshmallow or sandpaper, waxed paper, and wrapping paper)

3 Color Recognition

TIME: 10 minutes

Learning happens when: your child learns a song-game about colors. Tell him to look at his own clothes as you sing this song (sung to the tune of "If You're Happy and You Know It"):

Do your clothes have any red, any red?

Do your clothes have any red, any red?

If your clothes have any red, put your finger on your head,

If your clothes have any red, any red.

Do your clothes have any blue, any blue?

Do your clothes have any blue, any blue?

If your clothes have any blue, put your finger on your shoe,

If your clothes have any blue, any blue.

Do your clothes have any green, any green?

Do your clothes have any green, any green?

If your clothes have any green, wave your hand so you can be seen,

If your clothes have any green, any green.

Do your clothes have any yellow, any yellow?

Do your clothes have any yellow, any yellow?

If your clothes have any yellow, smile like a happy fellow,

If your clothes have any yellow, any yellow.

Do your clothes have any brown, any brown?

Do your clothes have any brown, any brown?

If your clothes have any brown, turn your smile into a frown,

If your clothes have any brown, any brown.

Variations: Make color collages using pictures from old magazines or catalogues.

✋ Go on a color hunt with your kinesthetic learner and ask him to find five things that are brown, blue, green, and so on.

👁 Play a game of I Spy Colors with your visual learner.

👂 Teach your auditory learner any other songs you know about colors or read a story about colors (for example, *Frederic,* by Leo Lionni).

Mastery occurs when: your child can recognize four to six colors.

You may want to help your child a little more if: he can't recognize at least four or five colors. Start with a couple of colors and then gradually add more as your child becomes successful. Use the variation of the activity and talk about the color names as you point them out in daily life.

4 | Food Tastes

Learning happens when: your child describes the food using taste and texture words.

Variations: Try doing this activity while eating a meal together. You could include the entire family.

✋ Take your kinesthetic learner with you on a trip to the grocery store. Ask her to help you get the things you name from the shelves. Before you put each item in the basket, ask your child to describe its taste. You may need to ask questions in order to help her recall some descriptors.

👁 Visual learners can find pictures in old magazines and make taste collages, including sweet, sour, bitter, spicy (hot), cold, and hot.

TIME: 10 minutes

MATERIALS
▪ 4 to 5 samples of your child's favorite foods (chips, pickles, cookie, banana, etc.)

👂 Talk to your auditory learner about your favorite snack or meal. Tell her what you enjoy about the food; describe its taste, texture, color, and smell. Then ask your child to describe her favorite snack or meal.

Mastery occurs when: your child can describe the taste of some foods.

You may want to help your child a little more if: she is having trouble describing tastes. Ask leading questions about the taste to help your child find the best words to describe it. For example, ask your child if the food is sweet or not sweet.

5 | Smell

TIME: 10 minutes

MATERIALS
▪ vinegar, vanilla extract, rubbing alcohol, lemon juice, cinnamon oil
▪ blindfold

Learning happens when: your child identifies items using his sense of smell. Blindfold your child and put various aromatic substances (with which your child is familiar) close to his face so that he can smell them. Ask him to guess what substance he smells, and give him immediate feedback.

Variations: Cut slices of fruits (banana, watermelon, orange, apple, peach, and so on) and put one slice each in a zipper-style plastic bag. Blindfold your child and let him pick up a plastic bag, open it, smell it, and guess the fruit. Take the blindfold off for him to check. After the activity, eat the fruit as a snack and describe the tastes.

✋ Ask your kinesthetic learner to help you fix a snack that has a scent that is easy to recognize (for example, hot chocolate, popcorn, salsa and chips) and talk about the smells.

👁 Ask your visual learner to draw pictures using scented markers. As you look at the pictures, question him about the scent of different parts of the picture.

👂 Read your auditory learner a book about noses or smells (for example, *The Nose Book,* by Theo LeSieg). Teach him to sing this song (sung to the tune of "It's Raining, It's Pouring"):

> I'm smelling, I'm smelling,
>
> My nose is busy smelling.
>
> This is the song I like to sing,
>
> When I smell most anything.

Mastery occurs when: your child begins to identify substances by their smell.

You may want to help your child a little more if: he has problems identifying what the smells are. Try describing the odors to him during the activity. An easy scent to start with is soap. What does it smell like when you wash clothes or wash your hair or your hands? Does the soap have a scent? What about when you are cooking? How does it smell when you are making his favorite food?

6 Sounds

Learning happens when: your child goes on a listening walk with you around your neighborhood. Call your child's attention to various sounds that you hear. Ask simple questions about whether a noise is loud or quiet, close or far away, pleasant or unpleasant. Ask your child if she can identify what makes the noise.

TIME: 5–10 minutes

Variations: Use recordings of animal noises and play a game in which your child tries to identify what's making the sound.

🖐 Ask your kinesthetic learner to walk around the house and touch various things that make noises and describe the noises they make.

👁 Your visual learner should try to match the sounds she hears outside with pictures of things that make similar sounds. Write down some sounds your child identified during the walking tour and use this list when browsing through magazines with your child at home.

👂 Tell your auditory learner a story (for example, "The Three Little Pigs," "Goldilocks and the Three Bears," "The Little Red Hen") using different voices for the different characters. Ask your child to describe the way each character talks.

Mastery occurs when: your child can use descriptive words to identify sounds.

You may want to help your child a little more if: she has problems describing the sounds. Model the correct answers and point out other sounds that have similar characteristics.

Life Science

Your child will be observing plants and animals in life science. Talk with him about the characteristics of living things, such as what they need in order to live. Animals need food, water, and shelter. Plants need soil, sunlight, and water. When talking with your child, describe the various stages that plants and animals go through. For example, many plants start as seeds and then grow into full-size plants with roots and leaves. Animals start as babies and grow into adults.

You can incorporate your discussions into daily life; for example, you can talk about the need for water as you give water to a pet or plant. Sit with your child and look through animal books. She can learn a great deal just by looking at pictures of animals at different stages. Watch quality TV programs and videos about animals and discuss the details together.

Life Science Skills	Having Problems?	Quick Tips
Can sort living and nonliving things	Has problems sorting living and nonliving things	Sort various things with your child and describe some differences between things that are alive and things that are not alive.
Understands that living things go through stages	Does not recognize the different stages of living things	Sit with your child and look at her baby pictures. Put the pictures in order according to age and tell stories about things she did at various ages.

Life Science Activities

1 Bug Cages

Learning happens when: your child begins to notice insects. Help your child catch insects and put a few into the bug cage to observe for two or three days (depending on his interest). Let your child observe the insects, and discuss his observations. Ask him questions as you observe the insects—for example, "How many legs does it have?" "Does it have wings?" "Describe the insect's eyes." "How does it move?" Be sure to take the insect back to the area where it was caught and release it. You might list the insects observed and the number of legs the insects have. Repeat this activity with different insects for as long as the activity holds your child's attention. Read books about insects to your child (for example, *The Grouchy Ladybug, The Very Lonely Firefly,* or *The Very Quiet Cricket,* by Eric Carle; *Ten Little Lady Bugs,* by Melanie Gerth).

TIME: 10 minutes

MATERIALS
- bug cage (or a jar with a mesh top)

Variations: Catch and observe a small lizard or toad. Some good books to read include *The Mixed Up Chameleon* or *The Foolish Tortoise,* by Eric Carle, and *Frog and Toad Are Friends,* by Arnold Lobel.

✋ Take a walk outside with your kinesthetic learner and look for insects. Talk about what you observe them doing, their homes, the way they move, and the way they look.

👁 Read your visual learner a book about insects (for example, *The Very Hungry Caterpillar,* by Eric Carle). Talk about what insects need to live. Compare that to what people need.

👂 Teach your auditory learner the song "Insects All Around" (sung to the tune of "Twinkle, Twinkle, Little Star"):

> Ladybugs and butterflies,
>
> Buzzing bees up in the sky.
>
> Teeny, tiny little ants,
>
> Crawling up and down the plants.
>
> Many insects can be found
>
> In the sky and on the ground.

Mastery occurs when: your child begins to recognize some insects.

You may want to help your child a little more if: he is afraid of insects. Don't rush this activity. Instead read a few books to him that depict insects in a nonthreatening way (for example, *The Grouchy Ladybug,* by Eric Carle).

2 | Sorting Seeds

TIME: 10 minutes

MATERIALS
- 5–10 each of dried beans and peas (any kind you have on hand), pumpkin seeds, sunflower seeds, and so on
- sticky notes

Learning happens when: you talk about seeds with your child. Show her the assortment of seeds and name one of each. Ask your child to sort the seeds into groups. Count each of the groups and write the number on a sticky note and place it on the table next to the group of seeds. Talk about how the seeds are the same and how they're different.

Variations: Draw a simple graph on paper and ask your child to group the seeds by placing them in columns on the graph. Compare the totals of the columns.

✋ Ask your kinesthetic learner to fill a paper cup half full of potting soil for each kind of seed, push a finger into the soil to leave a hole, and plant two or three of the seeds. Observe the plants daily for a week (be sure to keep the soil warm and moist) and compare the plants. Depending on the weather, you may want to plant them outside and continue to observe them with your child.

👁 Ask your visual learner to match the seeds to pictures of the plant.

🔊 Read your auditory learner the book *The Carrot Seed,* by Ruth Krauss. Ask questions about the book to check your child's recollection of the sequence.

Mastery occurs when: your child correctly sorts the seeds, learns some facts about them, and can compare and contrast them.

You may want to help your child a little more if: she finds sorting difficult. Practice will help. Sit with her and sort a variety of things together.

3 | Mothers and Babies

TIME: 10 minutes

MATERIALS
■ pictures of animals with their babies—available at www.knowledgeessentials.com

Learning happens when: you talk with your child about mothers and babies and about their similar looks and behaviors. Ask questions to discover how much your child knows. Ask your child if a mother bear could have a baby duck, or if a mother fish could have a puppy, and so on. Why or why not? Ask whether babies are exactly the same as their mothers. Why or why not? Explain that baby animals grow and change until they become adults, just as we grow and change until we become an adult.

Variations: Take a trip to the zoo and talk about the common needs of all animals. As you walk around with your child, talk about the differences in the looks of the various animals.

✋ Play Memory (Concentration) with your kinesthetic learner. Glue pictures of mothers and babies onto index cards. Players match mother to baby (ewe and lamb, mare and foal, hen and chick, and so on).

👁 Read your visual learner the book *My Monster Mama Loves Me So,* by Laura Leuck, or *Mama Don't Allow,* by Thatcher Hurd. Discuss similarities between the mama and the baby.

👂 Make up a rhyme with your auditory learner that starts with "Mama Don't Allow . . ."

Mastery occurs when: your child begins to generalize the concept that babies look something like their mothers and that babies, like all living things, grow and change until they become adults.

You may want to help your child a little more if: he has problems matching mothers and babies. Try to do all the variation activities so that he has more exposure to the concept.

4 Rooting a Sweet Potato

Learning happens when: your child observes the changes in the sweet potato. Push four toothpicks halfway into the potato and place it into the glass container with the toothpicks resting on the rim. Add enough water so that half the potato is immersed. Place the container where it will receive adequate light, and maintain the water level so that half the potato is always in water. In a few weeks, roots will grow out of the sides and bottom of the potato, and leaves will grow out of the top.

Time: 10 minutes

Materials
- sweet potato
- toothpicks
- clear glass container
- water

Variations: After your child has observed the root system and leaves for a while, the two of you can take the potato outside and plant it in the yard. Your child can continue to observe the plant and discuss changes.

This activity is perfect for your kinesthetic learner. If you do the variation, be sure that you involve her in digging the soil and watering the plant. You may also want to eat sweet potatoes together and describe the taste.

Ask your visual learner to describe the changes in the potato in sequence.

Teach your auditory learner the old chant "One potato, two potato, three potato, four; five potato, six potato, seven potato, more!"

Mastery occurs when: your child can describe changes in the sweet potato using the words "roots" and "leaves."

You may want to help your child a little more if: she has questions about roots and leaves. Read some books about plants to your child (for example, *Growing Vegetable Soup,* by Lois Ehlert;

Pumpkin Circle: The Story of a Garden, by Shmuel Thaler; *Flower Garden,* by Eve Bunting; *Franklin Plants a Tree,* by Paulette Bourgeois and Brenda Clark).

5 Worms

TIME: 10 minutes

MATERIALS
- potting soil
- clear quart jar
- mesh lid
- earthworms (dig them up from your yard or buy some from a bait shop)

Learning happens when: you and your child observe earthworms. Fill the jar with potting soil, stopping about two inches from the top. Add the earthworms and cover the jar securely with the mesh lid. Place the jar in a dark place for two or three days and then look at the jar with your child and discuss the changes. You should be able to see trails left by the earthworm. Explain that this keeps the soil loose and is helpful because soil is made of a mixture of minerals, air, water, and plant and animal material. Talk about how some insects are helpful and some are harmful. See if your child can give examples of both kinds and share some examples with him. Release the worms outdoors.

Variations: Use ants for the same activity.

Your kinesthetic learner should help dig for earthworms if at all possible and help fill the jar with soil. Teach the finger play "I Wiggle" and ask your child to act it out:

> I wiggle my fingers,
> I wiggle my toes,
> I wiggle my shoulders,
> I wiggle my nose.
> Now no more wiggles are left in me,
> So I will sit as still as can be.

Talk about the way worms moves. Are there other things that move as they do?

👁 Buy a rubber worm for your visual learner. Ask him to compare it with the living worm and describe their similarities and differences. Use a magnifying glass to look at both the soil and the worm, and ask him to describe what he sees.

👂 Read your auditory learner a book about worms (for example, *Wiggling Worms at Work,* by Wendy Pheffer).

Mastery occurs when: your child recognizes worms and can describe what they look like, the way they move, and where they live.

You may want to help your child a little more if: he can't recall any information about worms. Choose one of the other suggested activities and see if another approach will help get him interested.

Earth and Space Science

Now's your chance to go outside and play with your child while learning. In earth and space science, your child will be learning primarily about earth materials and weather, and there's no better place to do it than outdoors. Talk with your child about the weather on a daily basis to try and spark her interest in observing the weather. Talk about the temperature in general terms: "warm," "hot," "cold," "cool," "raining," "snowing," "windy." Discuss the type of clothes people wear to be comfortable during various types of weather. Ask your child to describe what the sky looks like today. Talk about the four seasons by relating them to the weather changes in your area.

Earth materials are things found in nature, such as water, soil, and rocks. Examine, identify, and describe the properties of objects. Compare and contrast the properties of water, soil, and rocks.

Earth and Space Science Skills	Having Problems?	Quick Tips
Understands the properties of common earth materials	Cannot describe common earth materials	Ask your child to help with the gardening so that he can get his hands in the dirt. Working with the soil will help him understand its properties. Look for pretty rocks with your child. Start a collection with him. Some science stores will have beautiful rocks and minerals for sale. Allow him to buy one or two. Discuss with your child where water is found on the earth. Take a trip to a lake or river. Do some water activities with him. Working with these materials will help your child understand their properties.
Describes the daily weather	Cannot describe the daily weather	Have a quick, daily discussion with your child about the weather. Go outside and discuss with her whether the sky is cloudless, partly cloudy, or filled with clouds. Talk about the temperature, whether it is hot, warm, or cold. By having these discussions, you are showing your child how to describe the weather. Before long, she will be giving you the scoop on the weather.
Observes and describes the characteristics of the four seasons	Does not recognize the characteristics of the various seasons	Discuss the seasons with your child. Describe the characteristics of each one. For example, you may comment on the pretty fall leaves or how the summertime is so much fun because it is warm enough to swim. Use the season words when talking about the changes you see.

Earth and Space Science Activities

1 Weather

Learning happens when: you talk about weather with your child. Ask questions to find out what he knows. Teach your child this song about weather (sung to the tune of "My Darling Clementine").

Time: 5–10 minutes

What's the weather, what's the weather?

What's the weather like today?
    Tell me children, what's the weather?
    What's the weather like today?

Is it sunny, *(make big circles with arms above head)*

Is it cloudy, *(cover eyes with hands)*

Is it rainy out today? *("rain" fingers)*

Tell me children, what's the weather, what's the weather like today?

Is it snowy, *(act cold)*

Is it windy, *(move arms as though they're blowing in the wind)*

Is it foggy out today? *(arms out front as though you can't see)*

Tell me children, what's the weather, what's the weather like today?

Variations: Create a rap song about the weather with your child. (Today it was hot, hot, hot . . .)

✋ Ask your kinesthetic learner to go outside to check the weather and report back to you. He will begin to associate the way the weather feels with adjectives to describe it.

👁 Make a simple weather chart for your visual learner, using drawings or pictures that illustrate sunny, cloudy, rainy, windy, and snowy. Put the chart on your refrigerator and ask your child to place a mark under the picture to indicate the day's weather. Continue this activity daily for two weeks. Take the chart down and ask your child to count the marks to see how many days were sunny, windy, and so on.

👂 Ask your auditory learner to give you a daily weather report, perhaps at the breakfast table or at dinner.

Mastery occurs when: your child understands that the weather changes every day, and knows some words to describe it.

You may want to help your child a little more if: he has problems describing the weather. Ask questions that guide him to the answer—for example, "Have you looked at the sky today?" "Are the treetops moving?" "How does it feel outside?" "Is it wet?" Have him practice putting all the information into a sentence.

2 | Rocks

TIME: 15 minutes

MATERIALS
▪ magnifying glass

Learning happens when: you walk together outside and gather eight to ten small rocks. Ask your child to choose one rock to examine with the magnifying glass. Examine the rock with your child and ask probing questions to encourage her to observe it carefully for specific characteristics. Continue the activity until you've used all the rocks that you gathered or your child grows tired of the activity.

Variations: Instead of describing the way rocks look, try having your child describe the way they feel. Ask her to pick up one rock, touch it, and use one word to describe the way it feels. Continue in the same way until she has touched all the rocks. Look for ways that the rocks are alike and ways they are different.

Have her hold one rock in each hand and tell which one is heavier.

✋ Be sure to try the variation activities with your kinesthetic learner. She will benefit from all the tactile activities. You may need to continue the activity over several sessions. At the end, go for a walk with your child and replace the rocks where you found them.

👁 Encourage your visual learner to examine a flower with the magnifying glass. Discuss the new things that she notices.

👂 Ask your auditory learner to share her observations with her grandparents, a neighbor, a friend, or a sibling.

Mastery occurs when: your child notices new things about rocks and can describe them.

You may want to help your child a little more if: she has trouble describing the rocks. Spend more time on developing the necessary vocabulary by starting a rock collection and describing the color, texture, size, and name of each type of rock.

3 | Dramatic Seasonal Play

Learning happens when: your child plays a game by dressing to match the weather you describe. Describe a day using weather vocabulary and ask your child to put on clothes that would feel comfortable that day.

Variations: You can read books about the seasons to your child (for example, *My Favorite Time of the Year*, by Susan Pearson; *The*

TIME: 10 minutes

MATERIALS
▪ seasonal dress-up clothes (coat, hat, mittens, sweater or sweatshirt, long pants, shorts, short-sleeve shirt, sandals)

Seasons of Arnold's Apple Tree, by Gail Gibbons; *Sleepy Bear,* by Lydia Dabcovich) and then discuss the way the characters are dressed in the illustrations.

- ✋ This is a great opportunity for your kinesthetic learner to practice fastening his clothes using various devices, such as zippers, buttons, Velcro fasteners, and laces.

- 👁 Ask your visual learner to watch as you make an umbrella by tracing around a half-circle tracer and a candy cane–shaped tracer (both made from cardboard). Hold the tracers and let your child try to trace the shapes onto construction paper. Let him decorate the umbrella using markers and stickers.

- 👂 Exchange roles with your auditory learner and ask him to describe the weather while you pick up the clothes that would feel comfortable.

Mastery occurs when: your child chooses clothes appropriate to the weather that you describe.

You may want to help your child a little more if: he has trouble selecting appropriate clothes. You choose and explain your choices, relating them back to the weather.

4   Water

TIME: 5–10 minutes

Learning happens when: you and your child sing and talk about water. Begin the activity using the old rhyme "Rain, Rain":

Rain, rain, go away

Come again some other day

We want to go outside and play

Come again some other day

(Optional lyrics: change the third line to say, "[Child's name]'s friends all want to play.")

Talk with your child about the importance of water—for drinking, cleaning, helping plants and animals grow, and providing a place for some animals to live. Talk about the different forms of water: ice, snow, rain, hail, mist, and fog. Finally talk about fun with water: playing in the sprinkler, swimming, splashing, going on water slides, and playing with bubbles.

Variations: Talk about some bodies of water—for example, stream, river, lake, and ocean. Refer to the ones with which your child has had experience. Talk about the ways they were alike and different, and the activities you participated in while you were there. Talk about ways to help keep these areas and the water there clean.

✋ Give your kinesthetic learner two sheets of paper, safety scissors, paste, and old magazines. Tell her that she should find pictures of wet things for one sheet of paper and dry things for the other.

👁 With your visual learner, look through magazines (for example, *Ranger Rick* and *Your Big Back Yard*) and old coloring books for pictures of animals that live in water, and name them. If you choose to use a coloring book, ask your child to color a water animal.

👂 Ask your auditory learner to recall reasons that water is important to us. List her responses and add any that she may have forgotten. Ask her to tell about a favorite activity that involves water.

Mastery occurs when: your child can tell some of the reasons why water is important and some of the forms that water takes.

You may want to help your child a little more if: she doesn't recall some of the forms that water can take. Ask her to experiment with ice and describe the changes that occur.

Environmental Learning

Take advantage of your child's natural curiosity when supplementing his science education. The following are examples of everyday learning that you can do with your child in the course of your day:

- Talk to your child about his surroundings.

- You and your child can collect seashells or rocks and compare them for similarities or differences, or you can count, sort, and group them.

- When it's time to make dinner, ask your child to name the ingredients and the utensils that you use as you cook. Talk about the odors your child smells in the kitchen and the heat from the stove. At mealtime or when you are cooking, talk about the way things smell and taste. Compare the way foods look and feel.

- Talk about the weather and the seasons with your child. Point out the changes that you see as the weather changes or as the seasons change. Ask your child what changes she notices.

- Talk about the ways plants and animals grow and change, the way animals move, and the things they eat.

- Group or sort toys as you put them away and describe your reasons for the grouping.

Encourage your child's curiosity about her environment by answering her questions. Better yet, question your child while guiding her in ways that enable her to discover the answers herself. All around there are things to observe, describe, identify, and wonder about. Read books to your child about the world around her to help develop vocabulary. Watch quality TV shows and videos about animals and talk about them together.

End of Preschool Science Checklist

Students working at the standard level at the end of preschool:

____ Observe, investigate, and play with objects

____ Compare objects by finding similarities and differences

____ Communicate questions and observations

____ Group and describe objects using the five senses

____ Identify and describe approximately ten animals

____ Have some understanding of time passing (yesterday, today, tomorrow, now, seasons, etc.)

____ Describe the daily weather

____ Identify and describe some common earth materials

Preschool Social Studies 9

What a marvelous job you have! You are your child's link to the world. You are the main person responsible for teaching your child how to get along with others, how to act at home and in public, and generally how to be a good person. All these skills are very important for your child's success as she progresses through school.

Preschool social studies is mainly about making personal connections to the world. Your child will be learning about history, civics, geography, and economics. Though these subjects may sound daunting, your child is naturally exposed to them every day. Preschool history relates to people and events of other times. Civics is showing traits of good citizenship. Geography involves your child's being able to describe and locate places in his neighborhood. Economics is related to using money to purchase goods.

History

Simply stated, history is learning a story about people, places, and events from the past. Because a child this age learns best by associating everything with himself, it is important to choose activities that allow your child to compare the stories with his own life and experiences. You might talk to your child about Native Americans while at a Native American festival or when you see images associated with Native Americans, such as a tepee. Relating a real topic to a cartoon version of it (such as the movie *Pocahontas*) isn't taboo—this is guerilla learning, and whatever works works. Holidays are easy for preschoolers: "Remember when we went to the lake on the Fourth of July? Do you know why we went to see fireworks?"

History Skills	Having Problems?	Quick Tips
Can tell you facts about Native Americans	Only knows Native Americans from the movies	Read books about Native Americans that are based on fact (for example, *The Legend of the Bluebonnet*, by Tomie dePaola; *Star Boy*, by Paul Goble; *Dancing Drum*, by Terri Cohlene).
Explains why we celebrate the Fourth of July and things that we do to celebrate	Isn't aware of the holiday	Talk about beginning a new country after establishing our independence from England. The Fourth of July is like America's birthday, and this is how we celebrate it. Talk about how we are proud to live in the United States.
Explains some changes in the way people live now compared to long ago	Thinks that Native Americans still live in tepees	Talk about how all people change the way they live over time. Native Americans have also changed: they may live next door and dress the same as you except for special occasions. Tell your child about some modern-day Native Americans whom she may know. Compare the way we dress to the way the European settlers dressed and the homes they lived then to the way we live now.

History Activities

1 Colonial Times

Learning happens when: you read the book, study the pictures, and discuss colonial family life with your child. As you read, ask your child questions about what the colonial people did that is similar to or different from your own way of doing things. When you finish the book, have your child tell you some things the colonial people did that were the same and some that were different from what your own family does. Let him look back at the pictures, if necessary. Take a sheet of paper and fold it in half. Ask your child to pick an activity that people do and draw the way the colonial person did it on one side and the way your family does it on the other.

Variations: Tell the story of the first Thanksgiving to your child. Compare and contrast the way the holiday was celebrated then and now. Show your child a picture of colonial people and compare and contrast the clothing they wore with what you wear today.

- Turn your living room into a stage for your kinesthetic learner; you could have him act out the story from the book you read.

- Your visual learner might like to draw more than one picture of the similarities and differences between the people of colonial times and people who live now.

- Tell your auditory learner some of the stories of your family. Talk about how things are different now from when his grandparents were children.

TIME: 20 minutes

MATERIALS
- picture book about colonial life (for example, *If You Lived in Colonial Times* and *Stone Soup*, by Ann McGovern; *One Little, Two Little, Three Little Pilgrims*, by Lynne Cravath)
- paper
- crayons

Mastery occurs when: your child can identify several similarities and differences between the activities that the colonial family did compared to your own.

You might want to help your child a little more if: he can't describe any similarities or differences between activities that the colonial family did compared to your own family. Ask your child questions to help him describe an activity—for example, washing the dishes. Ask "How did the colonial people wash their dishes, and how do we wash our dishes?" "Where did the water come from?"

2 Native Americans

TIME: 20 minutes

MATERIALS
■ storybook about Native Americans (for example, *The Legend of the Bluebonnet,* by Tomie dePaola; *Star Boy,* by Paul Goble; *Dancing Drum,* by Terri Cohlene)

Learning happens when: you read the book and talk about the story with your child. Explain to her that Native Americans are descendents of the first people to live in the Americas, that they had been here many years before explorers came here from Europe, that they are still living here, and that they have a unique culture.

Variations: Show pictures of Native Americans in traditional dress and pictures of Native Americans dressed in modern clothing. Help your child understand that Native Americans had cultures here for many years and that they still live in the United States, but don't always wear traditional dress. Tell your child that traditional dress is only part of Native American culture; Native Americans also have stories, songs, art, and dances.

✍ Help your kinesthetic learner make a "buckskin vest" from a used brown paper bag. Cut through the middle of the large side of the bag, cut a circle in the bottom of the bag for the neck, cut a hole on each of the narrow sides large enough for your child's arms. Show your child how to cut fringe around the bottom by cutting lines. After your child has played awhile wearing the vest, ask her to recall some facts about Native Americans.

👁 Your visual learner can make the vest described in the variation of the activity or the version for kinesthetic learners. Depending on which story you read, ask your child to decorate her vest by drawing bluebonnet flowers, stars, or drums on it.

👂 Ask your auditory learner to listen to a cassette about Native Americans. Some good examples include *Myth, Music and Dance of the American Indians,* by Ruth Cesare; *Songs About Native Americans,* by Lois Skiera-Zucek; and *Arrow to the Sun,* by Gerald McDermott.

Mastery occurs when: your child can recall and tell you accurate information about Native Americans.

You might want to help your child a little more if: she can't describe Native Americans. Try checking out videos from your public library on Native American life. The following are some good examples: *The Legend of the Indian Paintbrush,* by Great Plains National Institute; *Hawk, I'm Your Brother,* by Southwest Series; and *Annie and the Old One,* by Phoenix/BFA Films and Video.

3 | Tepees

Learning happens when: you talk with your child about homes that Native Americans lived in long ago. Show your child pictures of different kinds of homes. Explain that different groups of Native Americans living together were called tribes and that the tribes had different customs. Tell your child that the Plains Indians lived in

TIME: 30–40 minutes

MATERIALS
■ construction paper or plain white paper
■ safety scissors
■ pictures of Native American homes (available at www.knowledgeessentials.com)
■ 3 plastic straws
■ modeling clay
■ tape or glue
■ straight pin

tepees because they were hunters and gatherers. When the animals they hunted moved, they could move their homes in search of more game and different foods that grow in the wild. Explain that today he will make a tepee.

Secure three straws in three small balls of clay and connect the straws at the top with a straight pin, making a conical tepee framework. Place these on the kitchen counter or table. Trace a curved line at the top of the paper lengthwise and another line at the bottom to match the top curve. Both curves should curve up. Ask your child to cut along the lines using safety scissors. Help him wrap the paper around the straw framework and attach it using tape.

Variations: Read books about Native Americans that avoid stereotypes and that are accurate. Some examples are *Knots on a Counting Rope,* by Bill Martin Jr.; *Good Hunting Little Indian,* by Peggy Parish; and *Death of the Iron Horse,* by Paul Goble. Tell your child which of these represent tribes that would live in tepees. You can find more information on the Plains Indians at http://members.lycos.co.uk/plainsindian.

✋ You could make one tepee together with your kinesthetic learner and then give him extra supplies to make another one, recalling the steps in the process and using the first for a model.

👁 Ask your visual learner to draw designs on the outside of the tepee that might help us know something about him, as the Native Americans did.

👂 Ask your auditory learner questions about the procedure as you work together; ask him to guess what he thinks the next step is.

Mastery occurs when: your child can identify the tepee as the home of the Plains Indians and knows why they chose the tepee as their home.

You might want to help your child a little more if: he can't identify a tepee. Discuss with your child how the Plains Indians needed to move a lot and needed a home that could be taken with them easily. Do the variation activity with your child.

4 | Independence Day

Learning happens when: you read the book with your child and discuss what people do on the Fourth of July. Share with her why the United States celebrates this holiday. Divide the paper into four equal spaces. Have your child draw in each space a picture of something we do to celebrate the Fourth of July. In one of the spaces have her glue the wadded-up tissue paper to represent the fireworks.

Variations: Introduce your child to patriotic symbols of the United States that we see around the Fourth of July, such as Uncle Sam and the flag, using pictures from books, magazines, or the Internet (for example, www.american.edu/heintze/fourth.htm). Tell her the names of the symbols and explain their meaning. Talk about the ways that you and your family celebrate Independence Day.

🖐 Work a puzzle of the U.S. flag with your kinesthetic learner. Explain the significance of the flag.

👁 Ask your child to describe the U.S. flag. She may need to look at a real flag or at a picture of one to do this activity.

TIME: 20 minutes

MATERIALS
- large sheet of paper
- various colors of tissue paper
- glue
- picture book about the Fourth of July (for example, *Celebration*, by Jane Resh; *The Berenstain Bears and the Missing Watermelon*, by Jan and Stan Berenstain; *Henry's Fourth of July*, by Holly Keller)
- crayons

🦻 Make an audiotape with your auditory learner of what she learned about the Fourth of July. This will be a lot of fun to listen to in the future. Teach her to sing this song (sung to the tune of "Three Blind Mice"):

> Red, white, and blue; red, white, and blue
>
> Colors of our flag; colors of our flag
>
> Soon it will be the Fourth of July
>
> And, that you know, is the reason why
>
> We sing about our country's flag
>
> Red, white, and blue

Mastery occurs when: your child can tell you why we celebrate the Fourth of July, and name some of the things that people do to celebrate.

You might want to help your child a little more if: she does not understand the reason we celebrate the holiday. Do the variation activity.

Civics

Civics teaches preschoolers about being good citizens and doing the right thing. Your child will learn to share with others, be a member of a group, and show respect to people and the parts of a community. An important skill for preschoolers is learning to be a part of the group at school while realizing they are also part of the larger group of the community. There are rules at home, school, and in your community that help make us safe every day.

Civics Skills	Having Problems?	Quick Tips
Plays well with others	Doesn't want to share toys with others	Read books about friendship and talk about them, trying to relate them to an experience that your child has had (for example, *Peter's Chair*, by Ezra Jack Keats; *It's Mine*, by Leo Lionni; *My New Sandbox*, by Donna Jakob).
Can identify and explain some safety rules	Runs everywhere lately	Explain the reasons that it is not safe to run in a store, house, church, etc. Talk about how other people expect her to be walking. Ask how it feels when she runs into something.
Uses table manners	Doesn't do well eating in public	Explain that good manners are a social expectation for everyone when he or she is out in public. Also talk about how we don't always use proper manners at home (for example, sometimes we eat in front of the TV holding the food in our hands). Explain that you will begin to use good table manners every time you eat out. Review the manners that you expect of her before you go out to eat.
Follows rules	Doesn't "play fair"	Talk about playtimes when someone wasn't playing fairly. Talk about the way your child felt then. Discuss the fact that all people have feelings and that other children will feel that way about your child when he doesn't play fairly. Use recent examples whenever possible.

Civics Activities

1 | Following Rules

TIME: 10–15 minutes

MATERIALS
list of school rules

You will usually be given a copy of the preschool rules at the time you enroll your child. If not, ask the director for a copy.

Learning happens when: you ask your child what the rules are at school. List the rules on a slip of paper. Read each rule and ask why he thinks it is a rule. Ask what he thinks might happen if someone broke the rule.

Variations: try this activity with the set of rules we must follow in other places such as the library.

✋ Your kinesthetic learner might want to act out each rule as he is telling you what would happen if the rule were broken.

👁 It would be good for your visual learner to draw a picture or symbol to represent each rule.

👂 Ask your auditory learner to tell you about someone who followed rules today.

Mastery occurs when: your child can tell you why each rule is important.

You might want to help your child a little more if: he does not understand why each rule is important. Try demonstrating what could happen if each rule is broken.

2 | Sharing

Learning happens when: your child learns how to share her toys with a friend. Have a friend come over to play. Take out some of your child's favorite toys and have the two of them play with them together. In case of problems sharing the toys, you should stay close by to help mediate. Model ways to talk about sharing the toys with your friends, being fair, and taking turns.

Variations: Read a book about cooperation, friendship, and sharing (for example, *Friends at Work and Play,* by Rochelle Bunnett; *One for You and One for Me,* by Wendy Blaxland; *Making Friends,* by Fred Rogers). Talk about the book and help your child relate her own experiences to the theme of the story.

TIME: 20–30 minutes

MATERIALS
- a friend
- various toys

✋ Involve your kinesthetic learner and her friend with sharing a basketball, jump rope, or hula hoop.

👁 Involve your visual learner and her friend with sharing a video game, paints, or a visually oriented toy such as Lite-Brite.

👂 Involve your auditory learner and her friend with sharing some audiotapes or even a karaoke machine.

Mastery occurs when: your child can share her toys without getting upset.

You might want to help your children a little more if: she gets upset when someone is playing with her things. Before the friend comes over, let your child choose two or three toys that she is willing to share with her friend. Repeat this activity several times so that your child grows more accustomed to sharing.

3 Rules for Safety

TIME: 15–20 minutes

MATERIALS
■ storybook on safety (for example, *Fire Safety,* by Pati Meyers Gross; *Daddy and I Go Boating,* by Ken Kresisler; *Too Safe for Strangers,* by Robert Kahn; *Staying Safe,* by Dr. Alvin Silverstein, Virginia Silverstein, and Laura Silverstein; *The Right Touch,* by Sandy Kleven)

Learning happens when: your child listens to the story and can identify dangerous situations in it. Ask your child to describe some appropriate safe things to do for himself. This should be an ongoing activity that you come back to several times.

Variations: Choose a book with a different safety theme. The books recommended cover a variety of situations and each should be addressed separately. They should also be revisited periodically and discussed often, so that your child can automatically take measures to protect himself.

With your kinesthetic learner, act out different potentially dangerous situations. If you need some ideas for different situations, you can find some at www.knowledgeessentials.com. Make sure your child knows the best thing to do for each situation. Let him act it out several times so it will start to become second nature to him.

The visual learner might like to draw pictures of what he is supposed to do in a dangerous situation.

Auditory learners will benefit from listening to the story and then telling you what rules would have prevented the dangerous situation.

Mastery occurs when: your child can identify a dangerous situation and demonstrate that he knows what to do.

You may want to help your child a little more if: he does not understand what to do to get out of a dangerous situation. Start with just one situation and practice it until your child understands, then start practicing a new situation.

4 | Table Manners

Learning happens when: your child practices table manners at a pretend meal. Talk in advance about how we should behave at the table. One of the first things your child should practice is to chew with her mouth closed and to keep her napkin in her lap except when using it. You can find a list of dos and don'ts for table manners at www.knowledgeessentials.com.

Variations: Read a book on manners (for example, *Manners,* by Aliki; *Clifford's Manners,* by Norman Bridwell; *Excuse Me,* by Lisa Kopelke) and help relate it to your child's experiences. Talk about the book with your child and then role-play situations that call for using good manners.

✋ This is an excellent activity for a kinesthetic learner.

👁 Your visual learner will enjoy this activity whether eating at home or in a restaurant.

👂 Take your auditory learner to a restaurant to eat and talk about how she should behave. Is it the same as when she eats at home?

Mastery occurs when: your child demonstrates proper table manners when she is eating.

You might want to help your child a little more if: she does not demonstrate appropriate table manners. Practice during a few meals at home until she is successful, then move on to the restaurant.

TIME: 30–40 minutes

MATERIALS
▪ restaurant

Geography

Geography is all about location. Your child is already well aware of her home, her day care, and probably her favorite place to eat. Your child will learn to describe where an object or a place is located—not by standard directions but by such words as "near" and "far." Your child will learn about how maps represent her surroundings. She will also learn how to identify common features in the local environment, such as street signs, roads, and buildings, and natural features in the environment, such as hills, mountains, rivers, and oceans.

Geography Skills	Having Problems?	Quick Tips
Notices and talks about his surroundings	Describes environment in general terms (for example, "over there," "there," "outside")	Walk in the neighborhood with your child and point out specific things, name them, and describe them. Take turns with your child and ask questions to encourage him to give more details.
Understands that maps help people locate places	Doesn't recognize a map	Make a "map" of your house. Touch the spot on the map that represents the area where you are standing and ask your child to tell you what room you point to next. Continue this with each room.
Can indicate position when you say a position word	Cannot indicate positions that you name	Teach this rhyme to your child, using your hands to indicate the positions: "Up and down, and round and round, put your fingers on the ground. Over, under, in between, now my fingers can't be seen. Hands in front, hands behind, now my hands I cannot find. Here's my left hand, here's my right, hands and fingers back in sight."

Geography Activities

1 What Does That Place Look Like?

Learning happens when: your child makes a visual model of a familiar place. It might be his bedroom, classroom, or even his favorite place to eat. Have him draw a picture of the place on a sheet of paper and color it. Talk to your child about details of the place that are important to include in the model. Important details are those that tell what kind of place it is: a bed for a bedroom, features of the bedroom that show whose room it is, and so forth.

Variations: Have your child use building blocks to build a model of his room.

✋ Kinesthetic learners will enjoy doing the variation of this activity.

👁 Your visual learner will enjoy drawing a picture of his room. He should include a color or other detail that indicates clearly (to him) that the picture is of his room.

👂 Ask your auditory learner to describe the way his room looks. Make sure he includes details and directional words like "beside," "under," or "over."

Mastery occurs when: your child can identify the different things that belong in a model of his familiar place.

You might want to help your child a little more if: he can remember only the large items in the familiar place. Try asking questions or giving hints of other items he could include in his model.

TIME: 20 minutes

MATERIALS
- paper
- markers

2 Map Skills

TIME: 15 minutes

MATERIALS
- map of your state that can be written on
- markers

Learning happens when: your child begins to learn about what pictures on a map represent. Before starting, point out to your child the major parts of the map and what they are, such as land, water (oceans and rivers), and mountains. Have your child choose a feature on the map and color it. Explain what the symbol means and talk about an experience that your child has had in an area like that one. Continue to discuss the map symbols that are on your map.

Variations: Take a walk through your neighborhood and point out different land features. When you get home, work on making a map with your child. You draw the basic map on large paper and help your child cut pictures from magazines that represent things found in your neighborhood; your child should help you locate these features on the map and glue the pictures onto the map in the approximate location.

- ✋ Your kinesthetic learner will enjoy doing the variation of the activity.

- 👁 Have your visual learner draw symbols from the legend on the map of your home state.

- 👂 Ask your auditory learner to explain the meaning of the symbols on your state map.

Mastery occurs when: your child can name at least three types of information that a person can find by looking at a map.

You might want to help your child a little more if: she can't identify information that someone can find on a map. Make the legend together and explain the symbols used. Use a box lid or cookie sheet and cornmeal or rice to make a map of your yard.

3 Location Words

Learning happens when: your child describes where an object is located in the room. Review the meaning of words like "near," "far," "up," "down," "over," and "under" with your child and explain that you'll use them in this activity. Have your child choose an object in the room and then use words to describe its location. It's your job to guess what the object is.

Variations: Try switching roles with your child: you describe the location of the object, and your child tries to guess the object.

TIME: 20 minutes

MATERIALS
objects in a room

- A kinesthetic learner will enjoy the variation of this activity more than the main activity.

- Your visual learner should draw a map to guide you to the object instead of giving oral directions.

- Read one of your auditory learner's favorite books to her; as you look at the illustrations, ask specific questions about where things are located.

Mastery occurs when: your child can accurately give or follow directions to an object.

You might want to help your child a little more if: she can't give or follow the directions. Give the directions step by step. Make sure your child gets to the first place before giving the next direction.

Economics

What subject can children understand and like better than playtime? Money! Children learn fast what money is and that they need it to buy things they want. In preschool, kids will learn about the basic concepts of buying, selling, and trading.

Economics Skills	Having Problems?	Quick Tips
Identifies coins and bills by name	Can't tell coins apart	Read your child a book about money (for example, *The Complete Book of Time and Money,* by American Education Publishing; *Money Book: With Play Money,* by Elise Richards; *Benny's Pennies,* by Pat Brisson). Match a real coin to the coins that are on various pages in the book.
Understands that sometimes one doesn't have enough money to get what one wants	Knows that money is used to purchase goods, but wants it right now	Read the book *How Much Is That Doggie in the Window?* by Iza Trapani; talk about the book and about how sometimes people save money to get enough to buy something they really want.
Understands what it means to sell something	Is shy about talking to people in stores	Role-play buying goods at different kinds of stores. Set up a pretend store in your child's room.

Economics Activities

1 What Kind of Money Is That?

TIME: 15 minutes

MATERIALS
- pennies
- nickels
- dimes
- quarters
- $1 bills
- $5 bills

Learning happens when: you and your child discuss the various denominations of money. Have him sort the coins and bills. When he has finished sorting, ask why he sorted the objects in that way. Ask if he knows how much each type of money is worth. Discuss the value of each type of money. Help your child put the money in order from the lowest value to the highest value.

Variations: Put a variety of coins into a small gift bag. Ask your child to reach into the bag and pull out a coin, then identify the coin by name. Repeat.

👋 Your kinesthetic learner will enjoy doing the variation of this activity.

👁 For your visual learner, cut pictures of items from old magazines, tell him the cost of an item (keep the price the same as the value of one coin), and let him show you the coin that he would use to pay for the pictured item.

👂 Say to your auditory learner the value of one coin and let your child show you the coin that represents that amount of money.

Mastery occurs when: your child can identify the name of the coins; some children may be able to tell the value of each.

You might want to help your child a little more if: he has trouble naming the types of money. Use the variation of the activity.

2 Buying

Learning happens when: you take your child to a store and let her choose something that she would like to buy. Tell your child the price and whether she has enough money to buy the item. Discuss the purchase with your child. Let her decide on what to buy. If she has her mind set on something she doesn't have enough money for, encourage her to save money until she can purchase the item.

Variations: Set up an area where your child can play "store." Write price tags and tie or tape them to items from your child's toy box or to empty cans and boxes from your kitchen. Give your child an assortment of coins (or play money) to use in buying things from the store.

👋 Your kinesthetic learner will enjoy the variation of the activity.

TIME: 20 minutes

MATERIALS
▪ a store
▪ money for your child to spend

👁 Make a money chart with your visual learner. Ask your child to glue the coins to poster board while you write the value next to the coin.

👂 Talk about choices with your auditory learner. Explain that we all make choices when it comes to spending our money. Ask her to tell about a hard choice that she has had to make.

Mastery occurs when: your child can recognize coins and name their purpose—to buy things. She should be able to talk about the choices she made in the activity.

You may want to help your child more if: she doesn't understand why we have and use money. Each time you buy something for the next few days or so, talk to her about why you needed to use money. Then try the activity again.

3 Selling

TIME: 20 minutes

MATERIALS
▪ pretend money
▪ snack items
▪ toy cash register

Learning happens when: your child pretends to sell snacks. You can act as the customer. Choose your item and then have your child tell you the price and check you out. He will collect the money. Switch roles with your child and let him shop. The prices don't have to be realistic—the point is to know that everything has a price.

Variations: Read your child the story *Benny's Pennies,* by Pat Brisson. Help your child predict what Benny will buy, and recall what he bought first, second, and third. Talk about the rhyming words in the story. Help your child count out pennies to pay for the items that Benny bought.

🖐 Draw your kinesthetic learner a picture of a piggy bank and give him an assortment of coins. Explain that you will say the amount of money that goes into the bank; he should lay the coins in the bank to represent the amount.

👁 Show your visual learner how to do coin rubbings. You'll need to tear the paper from a crayon and give your child one of each of the coins and a sheet of paper. Have your child put the coins underneath the paper and use the side of the crayon to rub across the coins. Ask him to identify the coins from the pictures he makes.

👂 Teach the following poem to your auditory learner.

> Penny, penny,
> Easily spent
> Copper brown
> and worth one cent.
> Nickel, nickel,
> Thick and fat,
> You're worth five cents.
> I know that.
> Dime, dime,
> Little and thin,
> I remember,
> You're worth ten.
> Quarter, quarter
> Big and bold,
> You're worth twenty-five
> I am told!

Mastery occurs when: your child demonstrates the role of working, then the role of shopping and recognizes coins used to pay.

You might want to help your child a little more if: he doesn't understand what to do when playing store. Give your child money to purchase two items while you are shopping at a real grocery store. Point out the price sticker and read it to your child; help him count money to see if he can buy the items. Continue to play store at home.

Environmental Learning

Social studies are always around us, and there are always ways to practice social studies skills. Want a fun way to let your child practice? Take her to the park. In that one place, your child can share, take turns, and learn to play with other children. She can also see when someone is happy and empathize when someone is feeling sad. Going to a store or a restaurant lets her practice her economic skills as well as appropriate behavior. Just living life is one big social studies lesson, so take advantage of it and enjoy the time spent with your child.

End of Preschool Social Studies Checklist

Students who are working at the standard level at the end of preschool:

____ Share with others

____ Identify types of money

____ Know and follow general rules of safety

____ Can describe a familiar place

____ Can give simple directions

Teaching Your Preschooler Thinking Skills

10

Beginning of Preschool Thinking Skills Checklist

Children start day care at many different ages. Three- and four-year-olds students working at the standard level at the beginning of preschool:

_____ Uses clusters of words and sentences to communicate

_____ Communicates needs

_____ Is curious about the world around him

Teaching your preschooler to think sounds like a lofty goal, doesn't it? You can help foster a thinking mind in your child by treating him as an active participant in a home where you explore "why" and "how" questions. The more opportunities your child has to explore ideas and be heard at home, the more likely he is to be an active thinker both in and out of school.

Teaching children to use reason and to think logically improves their impulsive behavior and social adjustment. Children taught this way are less likely to develop behavioral difficulties than are otherwise well-adjusted children who do not learn these skills. Of course, the way you respond to your child and act in front of her has the most significant impact on how she learns to think and communicate.

In a study of children from kindergarten through fourth grade (Shure, 1993) that was the culmination of twenty years of research to test ideas about thinking skills, parent modeling, and behavior, M. B. Shure delineated four levels of communication that we all use all the time.

LEVEL 1: POWER ASSERTION (DEMANDS, BELITTLES, PUNISHES)

- Do it because I say so!
- Do you want a time-out?
- How many times have I told you . . . !
- If you can't share the truck, I'll take it away and neither of you will have it.

LEVEL 2: POSITIVE ALTERNATIVE (NO EXPLANATION)

- I'm on the phone now. Go watch TV.
- Ask him for the truck.
- You should share your toys.

LEVEL 3: INDUCTION (EXPLANATIONS AND REASONS)

- I feel angry when you interrupt me.
- If you hit, you'll lose a friend (hurt him).
- You'll make him angry if you hit him (grab toys).
- You shouldn't hit (grab). It's not nice.

LEVEL 4: PROBLEM-SOLVING PROCESS (TEACHING THINKING)

- What's the problem? What's the matter?
- How do you think I (she/he) feel(s) when you hit (grab)?
- What happened (might happen) when you did (do) that?
- Can you think of a different way to solve this problem (tell him/her/me how you feel)?
- Do you think that is or is not a good idea? Why (why not)?

The parents who communicated as often as possible on level 4 in Shure's study had children who were the least impulsive, were the least withdrawn, and showed the fewest behavior problems as observed by independent raters.

We all know that there are times when communicating on level 1 is the only way to go, so don't beat yourself up. You can't reason a child out of the street when a car is coming. Awareness of the communication levels enables you to implement the highest level as much of the time as possible, which in turn fosters a thinking child.

Teaching and modeling thinking encourages children to ask questions about information and ideas. It helps your child learn how to identify unstated assumptions, form and defend opinions, and see relationships between events and ideas. A thinking person raises a thinking child. That you are even reading this book assures you are a thinking person, so you are on the right track.

Don't expect your child's preschool teacher to stand up in front of the class and say, "Okay, it's time to learn to think." Instead, he or she will incorporate activities and language that foster the development and refinement of thinking skills, such as problem solving, concentration, and reasoning, throughout your child's daily activities. In the same way, you will foster thinking skills if you do many of the activities in this book with your child.

There are many approaches to teaching thinking. You can teach your child to use a set of identifiable skills, such as deciding between relevant and irrelevant information and generating questions from written material. This is particularly useful for auditory and visual learners. Your kinesthetic child learns to think more actively by participating in sports, hands-on projects, and similar activities.

Problem Solving

Problem solving is a hallmark of mathematical activity and a major means of developing mathematical knowledge. It is finding a way to reach a goal that is not immediately attainable. Problem solving is natural to young children because the world is new to them, and they exhibit curiosity, intelligence, and flexibility as they face new situations. The challenge at this level is to build on children's innate problem-solving inclinations and to preserve and encourage a disposition that values problem solving. You will find many challenging opportunities for your child to problem-solve in this book, particularly in the math and science chapters.

Concentration

Thinking skills begin with the ability to maintain a focus on one thing long enough to think it through. Thinking something through means understanding the information (in whatever form—for example, visual, print, or oral), questioning the information, and thinking about the alternatives before making a decision.

Concentration skills are a big part of learning to read. Your child's teacher will be working hard with him or her on concentration skills, and you can help reinforce these skills by trying the activities in the visual comprehension section of chapter 5.

Comprehension

This is a hard one. To think about something in a reasonable, logical manner, you need to understand it, but creative thinking is born from instances where you don't understand something. The trick is probably in the mix. Let your child explore new information and form creative thoughts about it, then talk to him logically about it. Giving your child time to think freely about new information allows him to think about it in many contexts and many forms before being told which concept or form is proper.

In order to better develop your child's understanding of different concepts, her perception should be shaped by touching, hearing, and seeing something simultaneously, to experience the concept as best as she can. Take time to let your child talk about what she is seeing, touching, and hearing. By experiencing new concepts in different contexts, your child can become aware of different aspects of an idea and develop her understanding of its meaning.

Reasoning

There is more than one type of reasoning. Formal reasoning skills, such as deductive and inductive reasoning, are developed at a later age. The reasoning skills that are focused on in preschool are more pre-reasoning skills than reasoning skills themselves: attention and categorization. This makes sense when you put it into the context of what Piaget's developmental stages identify as the abilities of four- and five-year-olds (chapter 2).

Paying attention simply has to do with children's being aware of when they are and are not attending to a task. You know what I mean! How many times have you tried to focus your preschooler on a certain task—say, coloring a picture—only to have him forget what he is doing the minute he sees something that catches his eye. It is important that your child begin to rein in his thinking and begin to concentrate so as to afford himself enough time to reason through more complicated thoughts as he grows.

Your child has been categorizing information since she was born. At this age your child will start to aggressively categorize more information than she has ever tried to in the past. *Categorization* occurs when learners classify objects or ideas as belonging to a group and having the characteristics of that group. It speeds up the thinking process, making it possible to generalize and to go beyond the information immediately given by the isolated object or idea. When your child looks at an animal and calls it a dog, she is categorizing.

Logic

Children learn about and understand logical concepts in different ways. In math, for example, some kids think about numbers in terms of where they are on a number line; other kids think about how many objects make up each number. These children reach an understanding of numbers, their meaning, and how to use them, but they reach it in different ways. Taking this example further, these children comprehend the information and understand what numbers represent. But if one group is then asked to handle the numbers in different contexts, the group will need to be aware of different aspects of numbers in order to develop a fuller understanding of their meaning. The group can then think about numbers in different ways and apply them to different situations in a logical way rather than simply recall what they mean.

A large part of logical thinking stems from the ability to see objects and apply concepts in many contexts. Teaching children to question information teaches them to think about the information in more than one context before making a logical conclusion about it. Logical thinking can be reinforced during the discipline process by applying a logical consequence to a behavior rather than using an arbitrary punishment.

Preschoolers are still figuring out the properties of objects and are not yet able to reverse operations—that is, to understand that 250 ml of water in a tall, narrow glass and 250 ml of water in a large, flat pan are equal in volume. Their reasoning, from an adult perspective, is still illogical. Things that happen simultaneously are thought to have a causal relationship to one another—for example, "Because I wore my new shoes, it rained."

Thinking Skills Activities

To help your child develop thinking skills, you can:

- Encourage her to ask questions about the world around her.

- Ask him to imagine what will happen next in the story when you are reading together.
- Actively listen to your child's conversation, responding seriously and nonjudgmentally to her questions.
- Ask what he is feeling and why when he expresses feelings.
- Suggest that she find facts to support her opinions and then encourage her to locate information relevant to her opinions.
- Use entertainment—a book, a TV program, or a movie—as the basis of family discussions.
- Use daily activities as occasions for learning (environmental learning).
- Reward him for inquisitive and/or creative activity that is productive.
- Ask her what she learned at school.

Environmental Learning

There are thousands of ways that you can use your child's everyday environment to encourage thinking skills. Remember, if your child is an active participant in a home where there are "why" and "how" discussions, he is more likely to be an active thinker both in and out of school.

End of Preschool Thinking Skills Checklist

Students who are working at the standard level at the end of preschool:

—— Communicate needs, wants, and thoughts verbally

—— Use complete sentences to recount an event

—— Ask questions

—— Follow two-step directions

Assessment

11

A key component to learning is evaluating what has been learned. Assessment serves several different purposes:

1. Assessing individual student abilities and knowledge and adapting instructions accordingly

2. Evaluating and improving the instructional program in general

3. Measuring and comparing school, school district, statewide, and national performance for broad public accountability

I know that you may feel overwhelmed at the prospect of testing a preschooler. The types of settings and tests used to measure preschoolers normally consist in large part of teacher observations on general and specific tasks. For example, many times there is a section of an assessment where your child is asked to draw something specific (a person or a house), and his progress is measured by the items he includes or excludes from the drawing.

There is more than one kind of assessment and more than one context in which this term is frequently used. There are multiple ways you and your child's teacher assess your child. There is broad assessment of your child's knowledge of certain things and her performance as compared to other children of the same age and grade. Standardized assessment is usually done at the end of the year (and most likely starts when your child is in kindergarten) and comprises many sessions of test taking in a short time period. There are uses for all types of assessment.

Assessing Individual Student Abilities and Knowledge

Your child's overall progress is assessed by considering her developmental stage and cognitive learning abilities with key concepts and key skills within the framework of her learning styles. Teachers (and by now, you) do this by observing your child on a daily basis, giving basic skills tests, gauging reaction and comprehension time when given new information, and asking frequent, informal questions. All the activities in this book include explanations for how to assess your child's performance, and the checklists at the beginning and end of the chapters can help you assess your child's progress in each skill.

Observation

Observation is the primary assessment tool in preschool. Observation as an assessment tool minimally invades your child's learning activity. At the preschool (and kindergarten) level, children's activities naturally integrate all dimensions of their development—intellectual, motivational, physical, and social. Teachers often observe your child in the throes of his activity and make notes.

Teacher notes based on observation are not, however, enough for a proper assessment. To make the observational assessment appropriate, teachers use their notes to place your child's behavior on a scale of developmental accomplishments—much like the developmental lists found in chapter 2 of this book. You can find some of the developmental scales that teachers use at www.knowledgeessentials.com.

Portfolio Assessment

Teachers have begun to implement portfolio assessment more frequently. Teachers are giving your child the opportunity to demonstrate learning through a variety of activities, such as art projects, directed play, and daily participation to determine the true levels of comprehension and skill development with the variety of materials and skills in each learning unit. Although many people think portfolio assessment is one of the most accurate methods of determining learning, it has been criticized for its subjectivity. Teachers try really hard not to be subjective; contrary to what some people think, they aren't likely to retaliate for a mishap with a parent by withholding smiley faces or stars from a child. When a child succeeds, the teacher has also succeeded. Discounting the child's success because of personal feelings destroys the teacher's professional success.

Teacher Ratings

Teacher ratings take the form of grades on older students' report cards, but from preschool through (many times) first grade, teacher ratings are more about social and emotional development than they are scores on activities. This makes sense in the light of Piaget, because teachers are trying to determine if your child is developmentally ready to learn certain things. The ratings tell your child's current and future teachers what types of information your child is ready to learn. You will be surprised at the validity of the teacher ratings even through adulthood. Did you get the rating "plays well with others"? If so, I bet you still do play well with others!

Preschool Assessment Criteria

All assessment tools used at this early age should satisfy certain criteria. Here are a few things by which you can judge your child's preschool assessment:

1. Assessment does not make your child feel anxious or scared.

2. Assessment information is obtained over time.

3. Information about a content area (reading readiness, for example) should be obtained from multiple activities to account for your child's learning style.

4. The length of the assessment is tailored to the typical attention span of your child's age group.

5. Assessment measures real knowledge in the context of real activities.

If your preschool's assessment activities meet these criteria, you and your child are on the right road. If not, you may want to discuss this with your child's preschool teacher.

Assessing for Kindergarten Readiness

The Big Question arises every spring: Is my child ready for kindergarten? Do late summer and early fall birthdays really mean anything?

You are right to be cautious. Today's kindergarten classroom has a serious curriculum that involves serious learning expectations and goals. Although there are many personal reasons for wanting to hold your child back, the truth is that you should look at your child's preschool assessments to determine if she is developmentally ready for kindergarten; if she is, you need to let her advance to the proper developmental environment. Starting your child off in the right learning environment will provide opportunities for social and academic success in the years ahead.

If you are grappling with the decision, consider the personality, temperament, and abilities of your child, as well as the age mix of the class he'll be in and the nature of the kindergarten program in your school district.

As was true when you were choosing a preschool, one of the first things to do is visit the kindergarten and find out what goes on in the classroom. Does the teacher focus on writing, phonics, and premath skills, or is the curriculum based on play and hands-on activities? It's also wise to talk to your child's preschool teachers about her strengths and vulnerabilities and about how she might fit into the program.

Another way to determine readiness is to have your child tested by an educational or developmental specialist. (Some school districts screen children as a matter of policy.) But experts advise parents not to make a decision based entirely on test results. Young children's behavior is very much dependent on the situation they are in, and testing involves eliciting behaviors in only one situation. What you end up seeing may not in fact relate well to what the child is capable of doing. Make the decision on the basis of the test as well as on information from preschool and kindergarten teachers, your pediatrician, and, especially, your own observations of your child.

Before holding your child back a year, it's also wise to consider the other options that may exist in your community. Even if a child is content in his current preschool (or at home), another year in the same situation might not be appropriate—your child may regress if not challenged. Children held back from kindergarten fare best in a pre-K program or in a preschool class of four- and five-year-olds that can accommodate older children.

The following checklists can help you, but ultimately the decision about whether or not your child is ready—is highly personal.

Kindergarten Readiness Checklist

Signs your child is a good candidate for kindergarten:

____ Likes following a routine

____ Gets along in a group

_____ Enjoys making friends

_____ Is able to choose an activity and stick with it

_____ Is able to sit and listen to a story

_____ Can manipulate a pencil or a crayon for drawing

_____ Is interested in looking at books and enjoys being read to

_____ Is interested in learning

_____ Can communicate needs to adults

Signs your child may benefit from being held back:

_____ Isn't comfortable asserting herself

_____ Allows other children to take toys or get in his space

_____ Lacks impulse control

_____ Settles disputes by hitting or biting instead of using words

_____ Is excessively anxious about separating from parents

_____ Has difficulty sitting still to listen to a story

_____ Has a short attention span (ten minutes or less) for projects and activities

Preschool Society

12

Preschoolers are working hard on their behavior and social skills and have a little society unto themselves. Each year your child will exhibit different social characteristics, and now that your preschooler is among the natives (so to speak) on a daily basis, you should start looking at the behavior of other children as well as your own child's to see how they can help or hinder your child's social development. You may at least want to know what to expect out of your child and how to deal with it. This chapter is designed to help with this.

Dress-Up

Remember playing dress-up? The completely outer-limits-of-your-imagination dramatic play in your head that you acted out on a regular basis? Vignettes of daily life, scenes from the past and dreams of being a grown-up? Playing dress-up is a popular activity among the preschool set. These kids love to pretend, and dress-up is all about creative play. They are having a great time and developing important skills that will influence learning for the rest of their lives.

What can you tell about your child's developmental age from his or her dramatic play? Children at the developmental age of four will start with themes that reflect their life experience. They play house, they play at being Mommy or Daddy. Simple props and clothes are fun for them, along with hats, sunglasses, an old adult vest or shirt, a scarf or string of beads, keys, and plastic dishes.

As children get older, their dramatic play becomes more wide ranging—and more social. Through fantasy play, they explore what it is to be another person in another time or place, and if they are playing with friends, they are also learning to negotiate, compromise, and collaborate.

Creative or dramatic play is important in all its forms. It stimulates the development of language and social skills, cognitive and imaginative development, and movement—all important aspects of school readiness. It also serves as an outlet for strong feelings and fears—for example, of doctor visits, fire emergencies, or being lost—that can be acted out with dramatic play props.

There are many ways to support and encourage creative play, one of which is to ask him to tell you about it. "What are you dressed up as?" "What are you doing?" You should observe your child to understand what he is interested in and then see what you can provide to evoke that theme. It doesn't have to be perfect—clothes and props are symbols for what children imagine. Some things are so versatile they're worth making—a cape, for example, adds a Junoesque *je ne sais quoi* to almost any character. Have a birthday coming up in your house? Try a dress-up party! Guests can come as a favorite character, a character they make up, or as Mommy or Daddy.

Enjoy your front-row view of your child's imagination at work—it is developmentally important, and because your child will outgrow it, the performance will most certainly be a limited engagement.

Temper Tantrums

You were having a lovely day. The sun was shining; you were at the park with your perfect child, who was playing with his favorite friends. It was a Norman Rockwell moment that you couldn't believe you were a part of. Then it happened. The earth shook, animals hid, a storm cloud centered itself over your head—and a four-year-old rained down on you. Your child just had his first temper tantrum. There is no way this is your child. No way. This child is naughty.

Four-year-olds' temper tantrums are not unusual. The world can be frustrating for children at this age. They live in the here and now, often wanting what they see without realizing that they can't always have it. Further, they think they should be able to do everything that they see other children doing. Developmentally, preschoolers are discovering and trying to master their movements and abilities. They expect to be able to do everything, so little things really do set them off.

Frustration leads to anger. "When children are frustrated, stress hormones start to flow through their bloodstream," says parent educator Mary Sheedy Kurcinka, author of *Kids, Parents, and Power Struggles* (Daria, 2000). "If the frustration continues unabated, those stress hormones keep building until they interfere with your child's ability to think straight." That's when your child is most likely to strike out— through such behaviors as biting, hitting, or screaming. It's also when you'll hear such dreaded phrases as "I hate you!" or "I can't do anything!"

One of the most important lessons our children learn, of course, is that they can't always get their way. For preschoolers, this lesson presents "an opportunity to resolve frustrating situations," Kurcinka says. "It's an important developmental breakthrough. By successfully dealing with frustration, kids develop initiative, autonomy, and a sense of capability. Faced with a challenge, they'll say to themselves, 'I can do it,' instead of becoming agitated and upset."

To help your preschooler better handle the frustrations she'll inevitably encounter, keep the following advice in mind:

- **Be on the ball.** "Think about the behaviors you've observed and heard your child express before she exploded in frustration," Kurcinka recommends (Daria, 2000). "The next time you see those physical cues, try to defuse the situation."

- **Time it out.** Encourage your child to take a break. Sometimes all I had to say to my son was "You know, you don't have to do it right now." Knowing that he could stop if he wanted to was often enough to calm him down.

- **Restart.** Don't be afraid to remove your child from the situation. Let's say your child took another child's toy away and refuses to give it back. Don't try to focus her attention on anything else. It's not going to work. Take the toy and move your child to time-out. After time-out, let your child give the situation another try or move to an entirely new setting.

- **Practice preschool Zen.** Know what calms your child down. Observe how he acts when he's upset. If he usually lashes out physically or hops on his rocking horse and rides, he's calmed by physical activity. So if he becomes frustrated while putting together a puzzle, for example, suggest that he play in the backyard for a little while instead. On the other hand, if your child typically pulls away from you when he's upset, then give him some quiet time, Kurcinka recommends. You may feel shunned, but your child needs to cool off. If you let him do that, he'll be ready to reconnect with you much faster.

- **Set boundaries.** Your next trip to the grocery store, mall, or park will be much easier for you and your child if you establish a few ground rules at the outset. For example, tell her that she can get ice cream from the truck only on weekend afternoons. Let her know that you will not buy any toys when you go to the mall.

Before you even walk into a supermarket, tell her you will not be buying any candy.

- **Go with the flow.** Don't shield your child from every frustrating situation. The frustration that kids experience can't be eliminated completely—nor would you want it to be, as it is an important part of the learning experience. Experts say that preschoolers need to learn to work through their frustrations. That means slowing down and allowing them time to figure things out on their own.

- **Back off.** Although you can make certain tasks easier by offering to help out, you should never jump in and take over. Don't try to complete a task simply because you don't want to spend the time it will take for your child to do it himself. If that happens, set aside another block of time when you will feel more patient to let your child complete the task.

Remember that the more you let your child do for herself, the more capable she will feel. That means she will feel less frustrated the next time a challenge presents itself. Slowly but surely, you will defuse those tantrums at their source, and the sun will shine on you once again.

Copy Cat

Did you start out with a child and end up with a parrot? If your child is copying your movements, words, and voice (and other people's too), then you have a child who is developmentally right on track.

Mimicking is a four-year-old behavior that is a necessary evil. Your child is learning social skills, language skills, communication processes, and perhaps behaviors that you wish had gone unseen. Everyone is an unwitting behavior model for your four-year–old, and the sooner you realize it, the sooner you can take control of the situation.

How do you take control of a four-year-old mimic? You try to place your child in the company of children and adults whom you would like your child to imitate. Sounds logical, right? It isn't as easy as it may seem. There are parts of your child's day that you can't control, particularly if he is in preschool. Let's start with the parts of your child's day that you do control.

Your child spends a lot of time around you and your family. You are all modeling behavior, and your four-year-old is watching. The easiest way to encourage nice behavior is to be nice in front of your child. Want your child to be considerate? You be considerate. A polite child has seen polite behavior. You can see where this is going—you are, as always, your child's most important teacher, and you need to apply that in all areas of your life, not just during "learning time."

The parts of your child's day that you can't control are dicey and interesting sources of information. Dicey because your child may be around children who exhibit poor behavior. Interesting because it enables you to see what is making an impression on your child. This is a golden opportunity to observe what kind of behavior is having an impact on your child and the sources of that behavior. Think of this as a blueprint of the friends your child will have during her teenage years and then decide if you want to skew your child's preferences toward milder (or more outgoing) behavior.

Separation Anxiety

Mommmmmmmyyyyyyyyy!!!!!

Separation anxiety got you down? The biggest bummer is that it is February and you thought that after you and your child made it through September that you would both be used to the whole drop-off-in-the-morning-thing. Why would your child start this all over again? There are lots of reasons why, and here are a few of them:

- **Holidays.** Changes in schedules and exciting events characterize your child's holidays. Preschoolers thrive on routine, so even though the holidays are fun and special, they disrupt your child's schedule and can easily cause setbacks with separation anxiety, potty time, and other milestones that your child has recently achieved.

- **Birth of a sibling.** Happy events shouldn't be traumatic, but if you are currently or have recently added to your family, you have probably already seen some anxiety in your preschooler. He is concerned about his place in the family, and that can translate into behavior regression. Be patient with your little one and continue with your child's normal schedule as much as possible. This too shall pass . . .

- **Being sick.** If your child has been ill and out of school, her routine has been disrupted and that is the key trigger for separation anxiety at school. She has been home (or at Grandma's, for example) and the center of loving care. Your child may be excited to get back to school and anxious at the same time.

- **Stress.** The key to all situations described here is stress in your child's daily life. Good stress (holidays) and bad stress (illness) can produce the same result: behavior regression such as separation anxiety. Any stressful situation at home or school can affect your preschooler's behavior, and your role is to identify what is going on while dealing with it in a way that reassures your child without letting the regressive behavior remain.

Separation anxiety can actually do your child some good by helping your child bond with his teacher. When children cry or have a hard time at school, teachers comfort them and let them know that they are not alone and that their parents have left them in a place where people are there to care for them. If your child is having a rough morning, don't hesitate to ask your child's teacher to throw some extra attention his way.

The strategy for dealing with separation anxiety is different at different times of the school year. In September (or in the first few weeks of school) it is appropriate to stay for a while with your child and gradually leave earlier each day. If your child has a relapse during the school year it is better not to stay and sneak out when your child is distracted. At this point in the year your child is not experiencing anxiety about going to a new place with a new teacher, but rather is experiencing anxiety about leaving you. There is a big difference between those sources of anxiety, and you can't go sneaking out when your child is worried about missing you. You should firmly tell your child that you will stay for five minutes and then kiss, hug, and tell him goodbye when you are leaving. It may be difficult at that moment, but you are showing your child that he can trust what you say—particularly when you say that you will be back later in the day to pick him up.

It is important to communicate clearly with your child during these episodes. Acknowledge your child's feelings, but make it clear that he has to stay at school. Assure him that he will be fine and that you will be back, using descriptions that he can relate to such as, "I'll pick you up after your story time" or "I'll see you when you've finished your second snack."

You are probably thinking, "Great, you are telling me how to help my child, but I really feel guilty about leaving him when he is crying." Yes, you do feel guilty and that is totally normal. For the sake of your child, try your best to keep your cool even as he loses his. Your emotions will fuel your child's fears, anxiety, or sense of security and well-being. Wouldn't it be great if you only fueled the latter? You can do that by keeping your wits about you and not showing your child how bad you feel every time he feels bad. These are tough lessons for you and your child, but I have confidence that both of you will be just fine.

Preschoolers are fun and challenging. We have only scratched the surface of what you will be seeing from your social butterfly. Enjoy this moment in time and the uniqueness that it represents. It's the bonus that comes with parenthood, and you are lucky to get this bonus tax-free.

Moving On to Kindergarten

13

You made it! Your preschooler is now going to be a kindergartner, and you are going to be the parent of a kindergartner! You can monitor your child's readiness for kindergarten and determine areas that you can help your child reinforce with the following subject area and developmental checklists.

Ready to Go

Students who are ready to go on to kindergarten:

Reading Readiness

____ Know words have meanings

____ Know letters make words

____ Know all or part of the alphabet

____ Know most of the sounds each letter makes

____ Recognize familiar written words, such as their name

____ Recognize written words found in their daily environment

Writing Readiness

____ Follow simple rules and instructions

____ Use a variety of strategies to problem-solve in class

____ Initiate activities in the classroom

____ Communicate needs, wants, and thoughts in primary language

____ Pay attention during teacher-directed group activities

____ Begin to make letter-sound associations

____ Engage in conversation (complete sentences, turn-taking)

____ Can recall activities and explain sequences of events

____ Participate in art activities that involve eye-hand coordination

____ Recognize own name in print

____ Persist with self-selected emergent writing activity

____ Appropriately express range of emotions

____ Begin to recognize signs in the environment

____ Try to copy words

____ Use letter-like forms, scribbles, or random letters to write messages

Math

____ Will recognize some numerals

____ Count orally to five

____ Recognize shapes—circle, square, triangle, rectangle

____ Compare, describe, and order objects by size

____ Compare sets of objects and describe them as "more" or "less"

____ Measure objects using informal measurement

____ Begin to understand some time concepts (yesterday, today, tomorrow)

Science

____ Observe, investigate, and play with objects

____ Compare objects by finding similarities and differences

____ Communicate questions and observations

____ Group and describe objects using the five senses

____ Identify and describe approximately ten animals

____ Have some understanding of time passing (yesterday, today, tomorrow, now, seasons, etc.)

____ Describe the daily weather

____ Identify and describe some common earth materials

Social Studies

____ Share with others

____ Identify types of money

____ Know and follow general rules of safety

____ Can describe a familiar place

____ Can give simple directions

Summertime

Congratulations! You made it through a very important year of skill building. Reinforce your child's new skills every chance you get so that she doesn't lose any of the skills she learned this past year. Each one is important to build on for future learning. Continue to use everyday activities to reinforce the skills your child has already learned. Summer is a great time to go to the public library. Most libraries have special summer programs with fun activities and special shows. Encourage creative thinking by providing fun art activities as well as a few "learning" field trips. By the time fall rolls around, your child will be more than ready for kindergarten.

LITERATURE FOR PRESCHOOLERS

This section contains a list of books that your child may find interesting, and learning activities along with the reading selections. You can find more recommended literature for your preschool child at www.knowledgeessentials.com.

Grandfather's Journey

Author: Allen Say

Publisher: Houghton Mifflin/Walter Lorraine Books

In this story about immigration and acculturation, home becomes an intangible place. The story is told through old pictures and family tales. Both the narrator and his grandfather would like to return to Japan, but when they do, they feel confused. As soon as they are in Japan, they are homesick for America.

Special Considerations: None.

Learning: Your child is learning about families and that many families in America came from families that live in other countries.

Activity: This is a good time to look through the family photo album and explain family relationships to your child (for example, cousins, grandparents, uncles, aunts).

Knuffle Bunny: A Cautionary Tale

Author: Mo Williams

Publisher: Hyperion

This book is about a little girl who loses her cherished stuffed bunny. Her father cannot understand what she is saying when she explains that the bunny has been left behind. Her mother instantly understands, and the family must retrace their activities to find the missing bunny.

Special Considerations: You will have to read this book to your child.

Learning: This is a great story to teach a child ways to express his feelings.

Activity: Talk about a time when your child lost or misplaced a favorite toy. Talk about the way he felt at the time.

Little Kitten's First Full Moon

Author: Keven Henkes

Publisher: Greenwillow

This story concerns a kitten that believes the moon is actually a bowl of milk. In an effort to lick the milk, she ends up with a bug in her mouth. Next, she jumps into the air trying to reach the milk, only to fall down the stairs. Again and again, the kitten's attempts to reach the moon lead to much frustration and exhaustion. There are repetitive phrases that introduce each attempt to get the milk along with rhythmic text and fun artwork.

Special Considerations: None.

Learning: Talk about how the shape of the full moon and the shape of the top of a bowl are both circles. Look through the book together for other circles.

Activity: Walk through the house together and find other things that are shaped like circles.

My Friend Rabbit

Author: Eric Rohmann
Publisher: Roaring Brook

Rabbit launches his toy airplane with his friend Mouse in the pilot seat. Rabbit promises Mouse that he can come up with a plan to get it down. He stacks animals on top of one another, starting with an elephant, until they are within reach of the airplane. Children will enjoy the expressive pictures of the animals and the minimal text.

Special Considerations: None.

Learning: Talk about friendship with your child. Ask her questions about her friends, what things they do together, how they treat each other, why she likes a friend.

Activity: Role-play being a good friend using puppets or stuffed animals. You be one friend and your child the other. Brainstorm a list of things that good friends do, and write the list as your child talks to you.

One Red Dot: A Pop-Up Book for Children of All Ages

Author: David A. Carter
Publisher: Little Simon

This book is a virtual game of hide-and-seek. Each pop-up page has a hidden red dot for the child to find. The book also encompasses numbering from one to ten and using primary colors.

Special Considerations: You will need to encourage your child to be gentle with book, so as not to damage the pop-ups.

Learning: Have your child locate all the red dots. Ask him to identify other primary colors used in the book and count objects in color together.

Activity: Make your own hide-and-seek book. Hide gold stars among the pages of any picture book and have your child find them. After he finds the stars, go back and count how many were hidden.

The Other Side
Author: Istvan Banyai
Publisher: Chronicle Books

This is an illustrated book that encourages a child to expand her perception of things. For example, there is an illustration of a boy looking out a window amid the chaos of his room. The next illustration shows the boy from the outside perspective, among the orderly windows of his apartment building. This book will help your child with understanding that things are not always as they seem.

Special Considerations: None.

Learning: Look at the book with your child and ask her to predict what will be on the next page. When the predictions do not match the next illustration, discuss it with your child and explore her perceptions.

Activity: Take your child on a walk around the neighborhood. Observe some permanent fixture in your neighborhood from different perspectives and talk about the differences in the way the object looks from different viewpoints. Take a photograph using a disposable camera. Look at the photos later and compare the way the object looks. Ask your child to recall where the two of you were standing when you took the photo.

Song and Dance Man
Author: Karen Ackerman
Publisher: Dragonfly Books

Grandpa reclaims his youth and profession as a song and dance man before the eyes of his three grandchildren. He dresses up in his old clothes left over from his vaudeville days and performs tricks, plays the banjo, and tells jokes. With wonderful illustrations, this book is perfect for preschoolers.

Special Considerations: None.

Learning: Ask your child to tell you what he knows about jobs. This will guide you in talking about jobs with your child. Ask, "What is Daddy's job?" "What is Mommy's job?" Explain that there are all kinds of jobs; mention some other professions. Talk about some of the reasons people work.

Activity: Ask your child to look back through the pictures in the book and then tell you about a favorite part or parts.

Swimmy
Author: Leo Lionni
Publisher: Dragonfly Books

This book has wonderful pictures to help tell the story of a little black fish. He is the only survivor of a school of fish swallowed by a tuna. He develops a plan to camouflage himself and his new friends so they will be safe from their enemies.

Special Considerations: None.

Learning: Ask your child to recall the vocabulary words from the book that are related to ocean life (for example, "seashore," "ocean," "water," "fish"). Challenge your child to touch these items in the illustrations in the book.

Activity: Talk about the cooperation between the fish; point out how life is better for all the small fish because they could cooperate. Recall a time when your child cooperated with others to do something as a group.

Ten Terrible Dinosaurs

Author: Paul Strickland
Publisher: Dutton Juvenile

A group of colorful dinosaurs count their way down from an energetic ten to a very tired one. As they wear themselves out playing, their numbers begin to dwindle in a perfect way to introduce subtraction to preschoolers.

Special Considerations: None.

Learning: Your child is continuing to practice counting and the association of numbers with objects in this book.

Activity: Ask your child to use model dinosaurs to dramatize the book as you reread it.

Tuesday

Author: David Wiesner
Publisher: Clarion Books

In this nearly wordless picture book, the reader goes on an imaginative voyage. Frogs fly through the night air one Tuesday, using lily pads as flying carpets. These mysterious frogs visit a suburban development and leave a few startled eyewitnesses, some scattered lily pads, and a frightened dog. Wiesner's visuals are spectacular, and children will enjoy them.

Special Considerations: None.

Learning: Your child is learning to comprehend a story through pictures.

Activity: Take a "picture walk" through the book and talk about the illustrations. Ask your child to make predictions about the story.

SOFTWARE FOR PRESCHOOLERS

There are many wonderful computer programs for you to use with your child. If you don't know how to use your computer, I'm sure your child can teach you. This appendix provides a list of software titles that are appropriate for preschoolers.

Blue's Clues Preschool

Humongous

Children go on a neighborhood adventure with Blue and her friends from *Blue's Clues*. Blue's teacher, Miss Marigold, has several places for the children to visit in order to show that learning does not stop outside of school. Each place has something special for Blue and the children to bring back to Circle Time. Children will learn sequencing, listening, and memory skills.

Product Focus: Core preschool skills

Curious George Preschool Learning Games

Simon & Schuster

Join Curious George in playing arcade games. Help him find circles, triangles, and other patterns, shapes, and letters. This program requires listening skills and the critical-thinking skills that help build a foundation for reading. Children can play at their own pace and challenge level.

Product Focus: Critical thinking and reading skills

Disney Learning Preschool
Disney Interactive

This software promotes critical-thinking and problem-solving skills for preschool-age children; it also enhances memory, listening, and observation skills. Your child will play with Disney characters in Stanley's underwater world. There are printable workbook pages and flash cards to further help your child learn.

Product Focus: Critical-thinking and problem-solving skills

Dora the Explorer—Backpack Adventure
Infogram

Children can join Dora the Explorer in returning library books. In Backpack Adventure, Dora receives a new backpack from her parents and sets off to return her library books with Boots and her friends. Together they solve problems, figure out puzzles, and play games. The game has three difficulty levels, and children will learn a little Spanish as well.

Product Focus: Critical-thinking and problem-solving skills

Dr. Seuss Preschool
Selectsoft

Horton the elephant and other Dr. Seuss characters will take your child on a journey to help baby Elma Sue find her mother. This software encourages early math and reading skills as well as memory and listening skills. Children will learn about numbers, counting, letters, phonics, shapes, and colors.

Product Focus: Preschool math, reading, and memory skills

JumpStart Preschool
Knowledge Adventure

Children explore a preschool town and solve puzzles, play games, and sing songs. The program reinforces important preschool fundamentals, such as reading readiness, word-sound recognition, memory development, counting, and more.

Product Focus: Critical-thinking and problem-solving skills

Little Bear Thinking Adventures
The Learning Company

Your child goes camping with Little Bear! Along the way, she learns about constellations, counting, and sorting, and even rebuilds a beaver dam. The program has printable progress reports, various difficulty levels, and over fifty different educational games.

Product Focus: Preschool math and memory skills

Madeline Preschool Classroom Companion
Encore

Children will learn letters and numbers, shapes and colors, sorting skills, geography, science, and more through this program. They will visit the zoo, the bakery, the school, and other places. There are printable activities so that children can work away from the computer.

Product Focus: Preschool math, reading, and memory skills

Millie's Math

Edmark

In seven activities, preschoolers will learn fundamental math concepts: numbers, addition, subtraction, quantities, patterns, sequencing, shapes, and sizes.

Product Focus: Preschool math skills

Trudy's Time and Place House

Edmark

In five activities, students explore geography and time with Trudy and her friends. In Trudy's house, children explore the concept of time and build time-telling skills. Children will also learn about geography, developing mapping and direction skills.

Product Focus: Time-telling and geography skills

GLOSSARY

accountability   Holding students responsible for what they learn and teachers responsible for what they teach.

achievement test   A test designed to efficiently measure the amount of knowledge and/or skill a person has acquired. This helps evaluate student learning in comparison with a standard or norm.

assessment   Measuring a student's learning.

authentic assessment   The concept of model, practice, and feedback in which students know what excellent performance is and are guided to practice an entire concept rather than bits and pieces in preparation for eventual understanding.

benchmark   A standard by which student performance can be measured in order to compare it and improve one's own skills or learning.

Bloom's taxonomy   A classification system for learning objectives that consists of six levels ranging from knowledge (which focuses on the reproduction of facts) to evaluation (which represents higher-level thinking).

competency test   A test intended to determine whether a student has met established minimum standards of skills and knowledge and is thus eligible for promotion, graduation, certification, or other official acknowledgment of achievement.

concept   An abstract, general notion—a heading that characterizes a set of behaviors and beliefs.

content goals   Statements that are like learning standards or learning objectives, but which describe only the topics to be studied, not the skills to be performed.

criterion-referenced test   A test in which the results can be used to determine a student's progress toward mastery of a content area or designated objectives of an instructional program. Performance is compared to an expected level of mastery in a content area rather than to other students' scores.

curriculum   The content and skills that are taught at each grade level.

curriculum alignment   The connection of subjects across grade levels, cumulatively, to build comprehensive, increasingly complex instructional programs.

developmental delay   A significant lag in meeting certain developmental indicators or growth milestones. A small lag is not considered to be a developmental delay. Developmental delay is often considered as the precursor to the label "disabled" for children from birth to nine years old.

developmental disorder   One of many disorders that interrupt normal childhood development, such as autism, dyslexia, and Asperger syndrome. They may affect a single area of development (as in specific developmental disorders like dyslexia) or several (as in pervasive developmental disorders like autism). With early intervention, most specific developmental disorders can be accommodated and overcome.

high-stakes testing   Any testing program whose results have important consequences for students, teachers, colleges, and/or areas, such as promotion, certification, graduation, or denial/approval of services and opportunity.

IQ test   A psychometric test that scores the performance of certain intellectual tasks and can provide assessors with a measurement of general intelligence.

learning disabilities   Disorders that involve understanding or using written or spoken language. They cause substantial difficulties in listening, speaking, reading, writing, or math. Learning disabilities may occur with conditions such as emotional disturbances or sensory impairments, but are not necessarily caused by them.

learning objectives   A set of expectations that are needed to meet the learning standard.

learning standards   Broad statements that describe what content a student should know and what skills a student should be able to demonstrate in different subject areas.

measurement   Quantitative description of student learning and qualitative description of student attitude.

median   The point on a scale that divides a group into two equal subgroups. The median is not affected by low or high scores, as is the mean. (See also **norm.**)

metacognition   The knowledge of one's own thinking processes and strategies, and the ability to consciously reflect and act on the knowledge of cognition to modify those processes and strategies.

multiple-choice test   A test in which students are presented with a question or an incomplete sentence or idea. The students are expected to choose the correct or best answer or completion from a menu of alternatives.

norm   A distribution of scores obtained from a norm group. The norm is the midpoint (or median) of scores or performance of the students in that group. Fifty percent will score above the norm and 50 percent will score below it.

norm group   A random group of students selected by a test developer to take a test to provide a range of scores and establish the percentiles of performance for use in determining scoring standards.

norm-referenced test A test in which a student or a group's performance is compared to that of a norm group. The results are relative to the performance of an external group and are designed to be compared with the norm group, resulting in a performance standard. These tests are often used to measure and compare students, schools, districts, and states on the basis of norm-established scales of achievement.

outcome An operationally defined educational goal, usually a culminating activity, product, or performance that can be measured.

performance goals Statements that are like learning standards or learning objectives, but they describe only the skills to be performed, not the content to be studied.

performance-based assessment Direct observation and rating of student performance of an educational objective, often an ongoing observation over a period of time, and typically involving the creation of products dealing with real life. Performance-based assessments use performance criteria to determine the degree to which a student has met an achievement target. Important elements of performance-based assessment include clear goals or performance criteria clearly articulated and communicated to the learner.

portfolio assessment A systematic and organized collection of a student's work that exhibits to others the direct evidence of the student's efforts, achievements, and progress over a period of time. The collection should involve the student in selection of its contents and should include information about the performance criteria, the rubric or criteria for judging merit, and evidence of student self-reflection or evaluation. It should include representative work, providing a documentation of the learner's performance and a basis for evaluation of the student's progress. Portfolios may include a variety of demonstrations of learning.

BIBLIOGRAPHY

Bloom, B. S. (ed.). (1956). *Taxonomy of Educational Objectives: The Classification of Educational Goals: Handbook I, Cognitive Domain.* New York: Longmans, Green.

Brainerd, C. J. (1978). *Piaget's Theory of Intelligence.* Upper Saddle River, N.J.: Prentice Hall.

Daria, I. (2000, Nov.) "Help Your Preschooler Handle Frustration." *Parents.* Retrieved Feb. 28, 2006, from http://www.parents.com/parents/story.jhtml?storyid=/templatedata/parents/story/data/3089.xml.

Evans, R. (1973). *Jean Piaget: The Man and His Ideas.* New York: Dutton.

Kurcinka, M. S. (2000). *Kids, Parents, and Power Struggles.* New York: HarperCollins.

Lavatelli, C. S. (1973). *Piaget's Theory Applied to an Early Childhood Curriculum.* Boston: American Science and Engineering.

London, C. (1988). "A Piagetian Constructivist Perspective on Curriculum Development." *Reading Improvement, 27,* 82–95.

National Association for the Education of Young Children and National Association of Early Childhood Specialists in State Departments of Education. (2002). *Early Learning Standards: Creating the Conditions for Success.* Washington, D.C.: NAEYC.

Piaget, J. (1972). "Development and Learning." In C. S. Lavatelli and F. Stendler (eds.), *Reading in Child Behavior and Development.* Orlando: Harcourt Brace.

———. (1972). *To Understand Is to Invent.* New York: Viking Press.

Shure, M. B. (1993). *Interpersonal Problem Solving and Prevention: A Comprehensive Report of Research and Training.* A five-year longitudinal study, kindergarten through grade 4, no. MH-40801. Washington, D.C.: National Institute of Mental Health.

Shure, M. B., and G. Spivack. (1980). "Interpersonal Problem Solving as a Mediator of Behavioral Adjustment in Preschool and Kindergarten Children." *Journal of Applied Developmental Psychology, 1,* 29–44.

———. (1982). "Interpersonal Problem-Solving in Young Children: A Cognitive Approach to Prevention." *American Journal of Community Psychology, 10,* 341–356.

Sigel, I., and R. Cocking. (1977). *Cognitive Development from Childhood to Adolescence: A Constructivist Perspective.* New York: Holt, Rinehart and Winston.

Singer, D., and T. Revenson. (1978). *A Piaget Primer: How a Child Thinks.* New York: International Universities Press.

Willis, M., and V. Hodson. (1999). *Discover Your Child's Learning Style.* New York: Crown.

INDEX